A PILGRIM'S GUIDE TO THE

Camino

T0060733

Santiago – Finisterre – Muxía – Santiago

Finisterre Muxía Circuit

*Practical & Mystical Manual
for the Modern-day Pilgrim*

John Brierley

© John Brierley 2022/3

A Pilgrim's Guide to the Camino Finisterre (first published in 2001).

ISBN: 978-1-912216-25-3

British Library Cataloguing-in-Publication Data.
A catalogue record for this book is available from the British Library.

All maps & Photographs © John Brierley 2022

Printed and bound in Czechia
Published by

CAMINO GUIDES
An imprint of Kaminn Media Ltd
272 Bath Street,
Glasgow, G2 4JR

Tel: +44 (0)141 354 1758
Fax: +44 (0)141 354 1759

Email: info@caminoguides.com
www.caminoguides.com

MAP LEGEND: Symbols & Abbreviations

Total km *equiv.* — Total distance for stage
— Adjusted for cumulative climb (each 100m vertical +10 mins)
(850m) **Alto** ▲ — Contours / High point of each stage
< 🄰 🄷 > — Intermediate accommodation ➲ (*often less busy / quieter*)
3.5→ — Precise distance between points (3.5 km = ± 1 hour)
→ 50m > / ^ / < — Interim distances 50m right> / s/o=straight on^ / <left

.... — Natural path / forest track / gravel *senda*
▬▬▬▬ — Quiet country lane (asphalt)
═══○═══ — Secondary road (*grey*: asphalt) / Roundabout *rotonda*
══N-11══ — Main road [N-] *Nacional* (*red*: additional traffic and hazard)
══A-1══ — Motorway *autopista* (*blue*: conventional motorway colour)
+++++++● — Railway *ferrocarril* / Station *estación*

● ● ● ● ● ● — Main Waymarked route (*yellow*: ± 80% of pilgrims)
● ● ● ● ● ● — Alternative Scenic route (*green*: more remote / less pilgrims)
● ● ● ● ● ● — Alternative road route (*grey*: more asphalt & traffic)
● ● ● ● ● ● — Optional detour *desvío* (*turquoise:* to point of interest)
● ● ● ● ● ● — Primary Path of pilgrimage (***purple***: inner path of Soul)

🗙 ❓ ❶ — Crossing *cruce* / Option *opción* / Extra care *¡cuidado!*
🜨 ☼ ╪ — Windmill *molino* / Viewpoint *punto de vista* / Radio mast
.▬.▬.▬. — National boundary / Provincial boundary *límite provincial*
∼ / ∽ — River *río* / Riverlet Stream *arroyo* / *rego*
◯ / ∼ — Sea or lake *Mar o lago* / Woodland *bosques*
✝ ✝ † — Church *iglesia* / Chapel *capilla* / Wayside cross *cruceiro*

🚰 💭 🏪 — Drinking font *fuente* [⌂] / Café-Bar / Shop (*mini*)*mercado*
🍴 *menú* V. — Restaurant / *menú peregrino* / V. *Vegetariano(a)*
ℹ 🏯 ✕ — Tourist office ❶ *turismo* / Manor house *pazo* / Rest area *picnic*
✚ ✪ ✉ — Pharmacy *farmacia* / Hospital / Post office *correos*
✈ 🚌 ⛽ — Airport / Bus station *estación de autobús* / *gasolinera*
⁂ *XIIc.* — Ancient monument / 12th century

🄷 🄿 🄲 — Hotels •*H-H*** €30-90 / Pension •*P** €20-35 / •*CR (B&B)* €35-75
x12 €35-45 — Number of private rooms *x12* €35(single)-45 (double) *approx*
🄷 🄰 🄰 — *Off* route accommodation / 🄰 maybe currently closed
🄰❶❷ 🄹 — Pilgrim hostel(s) *Albergue* ●*Alb.* + Youth hostel ●*Juventude*
[32] — Number of bed spaces (usually bunk beds *literas*) €5-€17
[÷4]+12 — ÷ number of dormitories / +12 number of private rooms €30+

Par. — Parish hostel *Parroquial* donation *donativo* / €5
Conv. — Convent or monastery hostel *donativo* / €5
Mun/Xunta — Municipal hostel €5+ / Galician government *Xunta* €8
Asoc. — Association hostel €8+
Priv. (*) — Private hostel (network*) €10-17
[all prices average (low season) for comparison purposes only]

📄 p.55 — Town plan *plan de la ciudad* with page number
(Pop.– Alt. m) — Town population – altitude in metres
— City suburbs / outskirts *afueras* (*grey*)
— Historical centre *centro histórico* / *barrio antiguo* (*brown*)

Overview: There is too much paraphernalia in our lives – in an effort to lighten the load we have produced this slim edition for the Camino Finisterre. This has been made possible by the selfless work of pilgrim associations that have waymarked the route such that, today, we need only the barest information to get us to our destination. It would be difficult to get lost if we remain present to each moment and attentive for the yellow arrows that point the way to *Finisterre (or back to Santiago if you are returning)* – mindfulness is the key. Please take time to familiarise yourself with the map symbols opposite.

As well as the stage maps and descriptions this guide contains some notes on the history of the route as well as advice on preparation, both for the outer and inner journey. If you would like to access more detailed notes and advice on what to pack please see our website *www.caminoguides.com*

All of us travel two paths simultaneously; the outer path along which we haul our body and the inner pathway of soul. We need to be mindful of both and take time to prepare ourselves accordingly. The traditional way of the pilgrim is to travel alone, by foot, carrying all the material possessions we might need for the journey ahead. This provides the first lesson for the pilgrim – to leave behind all that is superfluous and to travel with only the barest necessities. Preparation for the inner path is similar – we start by letting go of psychic waste accumulated over the years such as resentments, prejudices and outmoded belief systems. Walking with an open mind and open heart allows us to assimilate the lessons to be found along this ancient Path of Enquiry.

We have been asleep a long time. Despite the chaotic world around us, or perhaps because of it, something is stirring us to awaken from our collective amnesia. A sign of this awakening is the number of people drawn to walk the caminos. The hectic pace of modern life, experienced not only in our work but also our family and social lives, spins us ever outwards away from our centre. We have allowed ourselves to be thrown onto the surface of our lives – mistaking busy-ness for aliveness, but this superficial existence is inherently unsatisfying.

Whichever route we take, our ultimate Destination is assured. The only choice we have is how long it takes us to arrive *buen camino*.

Notes to this 2022/3 Edition:

As we continue to navigate the current global climate filled with change and uncertainties we find ourselves in the unusual position of printing an update to this guide sooner than usual. That is why this edition has been titled the 2022/3, as it has been updated since the previous 2022 edition and will bridge us into 2023. We trust that, despite the inevitability of change, the information here will be more than ample to guide you gracefully to Finisterre and back again. Check the website under 'Updates' *www.caminoguides.com/ pages/updates* and please feel free to email *jb@caminoguides.com* with any changes you find along the way so we can keep these guides fresh and relevant for those who follow in our footsteps.

If you have used our guides before then you may notice that we have updated the fonts and symbols for this edition. Please see the Map Legend page to familiarise yourself with the new symbols which we hope will provide an even more user friendly experience.

The world will always be a changing and uncertain place. Aside from global events we may each face individual challenges at any time. However after the recent pandemic and in light of the current environmental crisis there is a feeling of 'coming together' for shared experiences and help. After years of limits to our movement and ability to be in the presence of others there seems to be a common thirst for both more engagement and more quiet reflective space. The camino offers both. For centuries many have chosen to set foot on the path as a solo pilgrim, only to find themselves anything but alone. The sense of community found along the caminos means that one is rarely alone, even if we choose and welcome time spent in our own company we remain a member of an ever moving community of pilgrims that becomes our 'camino family'.

So as we release this latest edition, our hope for these times remains in many ways the same as before. That we might move from fear to love. That collectively we choose to respect each other and the natural world that is our home.

The Camino is a global family that connects each of us to every nation on earth. The great insight of the First Nations has always been to remind us:

Man did not create the web of life, he is merely a strand in it. Whatever he does to the web, he does to himself... we may yet find we are brothers after all.

< The photo opposite shows a pilgrim walking a section of path between Negreira and Olveiroa with the ever present windmills on the skyline.

El **Camino Finisterre** *O **Camiño Fistera** The way to the end of the earth.* For the majority of pilgrims Santiago is their final destination and they simply aren't aware of – or haven't thought about continuing to Finisterre or Muxía. Others are caught within a tightening schedule requiring an early return home. Some squeeze in a visit by bus but this is no substitute for walking the path which remains one of the most significant of the many camino itineraries. The paths to Finisterre and Muxía provide an opportunity to integrate our camino experiences before we find ourselves back home in the fast lane. Of the 80,000 km of waymarked caminos to Santiago de Compostela this is the only route that leaves *from* Santiago.

While there is a plethora of guidebooks on the routes into Santiago there is a dearth of information on the way to Finisterre. Perhaps it is Finisterre's connection with its pagan past that has acted as a deterrent. This mysterious headland marked the fault line between a Christian point of reference to the east and a pagan orientation to the west. The rising sun over *Monte Pindo* flooded through the entrance door to the Christian hermitage of San Guillerme but its setting over the western horizon to the Land of Eternal Youth *Tir-na-nóg* was watched over by the pagan Altar to the Sun *Ara Solis.* In the medieval period the focus within Spain was narrowed on Santiago de Compostela but to the wider world that focus had always been westward. That is why references to Finisterre come to us from foreign travellers and historians, from Ptolemy of Egypt at the dawn of the Christian era to George Borrow in the 18th century.

Whatever the reason for its relative obscurity, the camino to Finisterre has gained in popularity since the first edition was published in 2003. Boosted by those inspired to walk *back* to Santiago from Finisterre and/or Muxía. The route(s) are over 100 km and thus allows the bona-fide pilgrim to apply for a Compostela. There is no reliable way to assess actual numbers arriving/departing Finisterre as most pilgrims will have already obtained a certificate from completing their pilgrimage *into* Santiago and won't seek another on their return. However we know that 202 pilgrims (0.1% of the total) were awarded a certificate in 2011 (the first year records were kept) and last full year (pre Covid) the number had risen to 1,548!). But it is clear the numbers actually walking the route to/from Finisterre and Muxia are very much higher.

A synopsis of the history, legends and myths surrounding this fascinating corner at the 'End of the World' *Finis Terrae* are included as a backdrop for those interested in their exploration. However, it is their symbolism and the mystical experience to which they point that really matters. Literalism can be a hindrance to a deeper understanding of our lives and our place in the Cosmos. The question is not whether the earthly remains of St. James lie buried in Santiago nor whether his master travelled to Finisterre to meet the spiritual elders there – what really matters is whether we can absorb and live out the truth of their core teaching of unconditional love and forgiveness.

Galicia: Historical Snapshot, Brief Chronology and Mythology:

What follows is not a scholarly or historical treatise. It is included as a context in which to better understand the land we journey through. It appears on a yellow panel so you can skip this section if you have read it elsewhere or it is of no interest. It merely seeks to draw together some of the innumerable strands that make the camino routes through Galicia so enduring and that has drawn pilgrims from every single nation on earth to explore the unique part it plays in the in the evolution of human consciousness.

Finisterre lies at the heart of the Santiago story and its mythology. As noted elsewhere, belief and legend should not be confused with the Truth to which they point. We may miss the point entirely if we only take the literal view and try and drag the mystical into the factual. The boundary between the physical and metaphysical worlds is nowhere thinner than along the caminos that thread their way through Galicia. Let's not miss the opportunity to step over the threshold into the experience of the mystical path.

• *Megalithic period c. 4000 B.C.*

History tells us little about the Neolithic peoples who inhabited the western fringes of Europe. However, evidence of their stonework can be found all over the Galician landscape and goes back 6,000 years as seen in the petroglyphs and rock art of 4,000 B.C. and the dolmens *mamoas* of the same period. These mega-monuments are dotted all around Galicia *(see p. 40 for Dolmen at Perxubeira – photo above)*. This megalithic culture was deeply religious in nature and left a powerful impact on the peoples who followed.

• *Early Celtic period c. 1000 B.C.*

Central European Celts settled in western Spain inter-marrying with the Iberians. These Celti-Iberians were the forebears of the Celtic Nerios peoples who came to inhabit Galicia centuries before the Roman occupation. Remains of their Celtic villages *castros* can still be seen around the remote countryside (see p.38 for Castro at Monte Aro). These fortified villages were built in a circular formation usually occupying some elevated ground or hillock. The extensive mineral deposits of Galicia gave rise to a rich artistic movement and Celtic bronze and gold artefacts from this area can be seen in museums across Europe. Galicia remains one of the least well known of the Celtic nations and yet it is one of the oldest. Galician Celts trace their mythic lineage to the king of Scythia in the Black sea area where the Druid Caichar had a vision in which he saw them travelling west to found Galicia and Ireland. The first

Gaelic colony was established in Galicia under Brath and his son Breogán the latter becoming the legendary hero who founded Brigantium (present day A Coruña) entering folklore and the national anthem of Galicia in the process, *'Wake up from your dreams, home of Breogán.'* His grandson became King Milesius after whom the Celtic Milesians were named. It is generally accepted that the first Celts to settle in Ireland were Milesians from Galicia. In a masterful stroke of genius early Christian monks then extended the Celtic lineage 36 generations back to link it with the biblical Adam!

• Early Christian Period c. 40 A.D

While there is no historical evidence to support the view that St. James preached in Galicia, there are some anecdotal references to that effect. The parish church in Finisterre has a fine statue of **Santiago Peregrino** (photo>) and a statue of Christ much revered in Galicia and associated with many miracles (see p.63). It would appear San Tiago sailed to Galicia, landing at Padrón, to preach Christ's message, his body being brought back there after his martyrdom in Jerusalem around 40 A.D. It is reasonable to assume that he, and his followers, would have sought to bring the Christian message to areas of spiritual significance on which to graft its own message. Finisterre was one of the most significant spiritual sites in the world at that time and it was inevitable that it would draw those with a spiritual mission. It was also accessible being directly on the sea route from Palestine.

• Early Roman period 100 B.C.

By the end of the first century the Romans controlled most of the southern Iberian peninsular naming the unruly northern province *Hispania Ulterior* to include the area known as *Gallaecia*. The ancient Roman city of Dugium (present day Finisterre) re-enacts the resurrection of Christ in a festival of 'national importance' each year at Easter (see photo). In 61 BC Julius Caesar became governor and conducted naval expeditions along the coast and finally wrested control of the Atlantic seaboard from the Phoenicians. In 136 the proconsul Decimus Junius Brutus led his legions across the Lima and Minho rivers to enter Gallaecia by land route for the first time. He met resistance not only from the fierce inhabitants but also from his own soldiers wary of crossing the river *Lima* thought to represent one of the rivers of Hades – the river of forgetfulness *Lethe*. Brutus became the first Roman general to make it to Finisterre 'by land' and was reputedly mesmerised at the way the sea 'drank up' the sun and was predisposed to the pagan and Druidic worship centred on the Phoenician Altar to the Sun *Ara*

Solis. The Romans perseverance in conquering this corner of Hispania was, however, more prosaic being primarily due to its rich mining potential. The largest goldmines in the Empire were located at *Las Médulas (see a Pilgrim's Guide to the **Camino Invierno**)*.

• *The Middle Ages 476 – 1453*

Hispania was the Latin name given to the whole Iberian peninsula. After the fall of the Roman Empire in 476 CE the north-western province (present day Galicia) was ruled by the Vandals, Suevi and Visigoths descendants of the Germanic tribes that had overrun Roman Hispania forcing its collapse. It is hard to believe (and much misunderstood) but the Moorish 'invasion' of the Iberian peninsula in 711 was actually an invitation to the forces of Islam by the squabbling Visigothic nobles to help in their domestic feuds. The Umayyad Muslims were happy to oblige and so the invasion by invitation began. Muslim forces quickly moved north to conquer the whole peninsular, capturing the bells of Santiago cathedral along the way and infamously taking them to Granada. But Galicia proved impossible to control and Islamic rule here lasted only a few decades. It was to take another 700 years before the re-conquest was complete in the south – and the bells returned to Santiago!

• *The Catholic Monarchs 1469 – 1516*

The marriage in 1469 of Isabella I of Castille and Fernando II of Aragón saw the merging of two of the most powerful kingdoms in Spain. The title Catholic Monarchs *los Reyes Católicos* was bestowed by Pope Alexander VI with an eye to aiding the re-conquest and unifying Spain under Roman Catholicism. This was finally achieved after the conquest of the Muslim Kingdom of Granada in 1492, the same year Columbus 'discovered' the Americas. This illustrious period was tarnished by the expulsion or massacre of non-Catholics under the infamous Inquisition initiated under her reign. Isabella is, perhaps, best remembered for her more beneficent activities such as the building of the pilgrim hospital in Santiago, now the luxurious *parador Hostal Dos Reis Católicos* – reputedly the oldest hotel in the world in continuous occupation for that purpose. Its magnificent Renaissance facade is one of the grander features of the Praza de Obradoiro. Queen Isabella's munificence lives on in the custom whereby a limited number of pilgrims receive free meals everyday!

• *The War(s) of Independence 1807 – 1814*

Despite its remote location, Galicia was not spared the effects of the War of Independence 'Peninsular War' (1807–1814) when forces of Napoleon ransacked many of the villages along which we pass through (see Hospital p.46). The war was a military conflict between Napoleon's empire and Bourbon Spain for control of the Iberian Peninsula. It began when the French and Spanish invaded Portugal in 1807 and escalated the following year when France turned on its former ally Spain and lasted until Napoleon was defeated in 1814. The Peninsular War overlaps with the Spanish War of Independence *Guerra de la Independencia Española* which began with the uprising on 2 May 1808 *Dos de Mayo. (still remembered in many a street name)* ending in 1814.

• *The Carlist Wars & First Spanish Republic 1833 – 1876*

Next came the Carlist Wars between King Carlos V and republicanism. Towards the end of the 3rd Carlist war the first Spanish Republic was proclaimed in 1873. Again the remoteness of Galicia was no bar to its involvement in anti-monarchist activities. Indeed its resistance to any outside interference continues to this day. No introduction to Galicia would be complete without mention of Castelao who was born in Rianxo in 1886 and who died in Buenos Aires in 1950. Politician, writer, and doctor. Identified as a founding father of Galician nationalism, identity and culture and president of the Galician Gelegust Party. He presented the idea of an independent Galician State *Estatuto de Galicia* to the Spanish Parliament in the same year that General Franco appeared on the political scene. Despite various initiatives to earn independence for Galicia it was not until 1981 that it achieved a measure of autonomy, being recognised as a separate autonomous region in that year.

• *The Spanish Civil War 1936 – 1939 & The Franco Period.*

In 1936 General Franco seized power leading to one of the bloodiest civil wars in history and its effects can still be felt today despite the 'Pact of Forgetting' *Pacto del Olvido* a decision by all parties to the conflict to avoid having to deal with the horrifying legacy of Fascism under Franco. The Pact attempted to transition from an autocratic to democratic rule of law without recriminations for the countless thousands killed summarily and buried in unmarked graves throughout Spain. While suppression of painful memories helped in national reconciliation at that time – these memories remain close to the surface and there is a growing sense within Spain today that it should now take a more honest and open look at the violence of that period in order to bring about a national reconciliation.

• *Spain 1975 – 2019*

After Franco's death in 1975 King Carlos nominally succeeded and appointed political reformist Adolfo Suárez to form a government. In 1982 the Spanish Socialist Workers' Party *Partido Socialista Obrero Español* **PSOE** won a sweeping victory under Felipe González who successfully steered Spain into full membership of the EEC in 1986. In 1996 José María Aznar, leader of the centre-right People's Party *Partido Popular* **PP** won a narrow mandate but in 2002 the oil tanker

'Prestige' ran into a storm off Finisterre and the ensuing ecological catastrophe sank not only the livelihood of scores of Galician fisherman but, in due time, the right wing government as well resulting in a popular cry up and down the country of 'never again' *nunca maís*. The socialists were now back in power under José Luis Rodríguez Zapatero but the economic crisis led to the re-election of the conservative **PP** in December 2011 under Mariano Rajoy. Corruption scandals led to a new socialist government who set in motion an immediate change in foreign policy and, more controversially, a sudden but decisive shift from a conservative Catholic to a liberal secular society that led to one newspaper headline, *'Church and State square up in struggle for the spirit of Spain.'* A new political alliance was formed in 2019 between socialist Pedro Sanchez **PSOE** and Pablo Iglesias 'United We Can' *Unidas Podemos* in part to keep the emerging far-right party **VOX** from forming an alliance with the **PP**! ... And seemingly immune to all these social and political upheavals, the *Caminos* go quietly about their gentle spirit of transformation.

Galician Culture: The flowering of Galician art that took place under Alfonso VII and Ferdinand II (kings of Galicia until it was absorbed into León and Castille under Ferdinand III) saw the completion of the great cathedrals of Ourense, Lugo and Tui, as well as Santiago. However, between the three great powers comprising the  Catholic monarchy, the Aristocracy and Castille; Galician art, culture and language were greatly diluted. Indeed while the French Way *Camino Francés* introduced wonderfully inspiring European art and artisans to towns all along the route to Santiago, it had the effect of diminishing the Celtic influences within Galicia. **Galician Nationalism** appears to be born more out of a deep pride in its traditions, rather than a need to overthrow a culture that has been imposed from outside. This is not unlike other Celtic cultures that have found themselves marginalised on the Western fringes of Europe. We demean Galicia and ourselves by stereotyping popular Spanish culture onto her. This is not the Spain of castanets, paella and Rioja wines. Her identity is clearly Celtic with *gaitas, mariscos* and *Albariño* wines predominating – all of which are a cause of justified pride.

The Revival *Rexurdimento* of Galician language and literature in the 19th century was spearheaded with the publication in 1863 of *Cantares Gallegos* by the incomparable Galician poetess, Rosalía Castro. The Revival reached its zenith in the 1880's with the publication of many illuminating Galician texts such as *Follas Novas* also by Rosalía Castro, *Saudades Galegas* by Lamas de Carvajal and *Queixumes dos Pinos* by Eduardo Pondal. Galicia's culture has been kept alive as much by its exiles, political and economic, as by those that remained behind. The unofficial anthem of Galicia, The Pines *Os Pinos* was written and first sung in South America where it urged the Galician people to awaken from the yoke of servitude into freedom: *'Listen to the voices of the murmuring pines which is none other than the voices of the Galician people.'* However, even the pine trees seem under threat from the imported eucalyptus that has taken over large swathes of the countryside. The fruits of this revival can be tasted, nonetheless, throughout Galicia today. You may well hear the swirl of the traditional Galician bagpipes *Gaita* in the bars of Santiago or Finisterre or at one of its many festivals and fairs that take place throughout the year. Many of these are based on the ancient Celtic celebration of the seasons particularly at the equinoxes and the summer and winter solstices. The short pilgrimages to local shrines *romerías* endorse the deeply held religious values of the people of Galicia such as Holy Week *Semana Santa* in Finisterre and drawing ever larger crowds are the secular food and music festivals.

Galician Language: The distinctive language of Galicia *Gallego* is still widely used today. The language institute estimates that 94% of the population understand it, while 88% can speak it. Galego belongs to the Iberian Romance group of languages with some common aspects with Portuguese. Phrase books between Spanish *Castellano* Galician *Galego* and English are difficult to find but one of the more obvious differences is the substitution of the Spanish J – hard as in Junta (pron: **kh**unta) as opposed to the softer Galego Xunta (pron: **sh**unta). Here are a few common phrases to help distinguish one from the other:

	Castellano	*Galego*
The Jacobean Way	Del Camino Jacobeo	Do Camiño Xacobeo
Pilgrimage	Peregrinaje	Peregrinaxe
Fountains of Galicia	Las Fuentes de Galicia	Das Fontes de Galiza
The Botanical garden	El Jardin Botanico	O Xardín Botánico
Collegiate church	Colegiata Iglesia	Colexiata Igrexa
Town Hall	Casa Consistorial	Concello da Vila
Below the main Square	Bajo el plaza mayor	Debaixo do praza maior
Holy Year of St. James	Año Santo Jacobeo	Ano Santo Xacobeo

Preparation – A Quick Guide:

[1] Practical Considerations:

• **When?** Spring is often wet and windy but the route is relatively quiet with early flowers appearing. Summer is busy and hot and hostels often full. Autumn usually provides the most stable weather with harvesting adding to the colour and celebrations of the countryside. Winter is solitary and cold with reduced daylight hours for walking and some hostels will be closed.

• **How long?** Santiago to Finisterre centre is 86.7 km and can be covered in a demanding 3 days (averaging 28.9 km per day) or a more usual 4 days (21.7 per day). Interim lodging allows each stage to be varied according to differing abilities, pace and intentions. The complete circuit back to Santiago via Muxia is 200 km. Allow 10 days for an average of 25 km per day and a day to explore each of Finisterre and Muxia.

[2] Preparation – Outer: What do I need to take
• Buy your boots in time to walk them in before you go.
• Pack a Poncho – Galicia is notorious for its downpours.
• Bring a hat – sunstroke is painful and can be dangerous.
• Look again if your backpack weighs more than 10 kilos.

If this is your first pilgrimage you can source more comprehensive notes on preparation at _www.caminoguides.com_

... *and* consider leaving behind.

• Books, except this one – all the maps and promptings you need are included.
• Extras, Galicia has shops if you need to replace something.
• Everything that is superfluous for pilgrimage. Take time to reflect carefully on this point as it can form the basis of our questioning of what is really important in our life and spiritual awakening. We have become reliant, even addicted, to so many extraneous 'things'. We need to de-clutter in order to clear space for what truly matters to arise in our awareness.

[3] Language: learn at least some basic phrases now, *before* you go.

[4] Pilgrim Passport: Get a *credencial* from your local confraternity – and join it (see p.95).

[5] Protocol: Have consideration for the needs of your fellow pilgrims, gratitude for your hosts and take care of nature and the Landscape Temple.

[6] Prayer: May my every step be a prayer for peace and loving kindness.

[7] Preparation *Inner*: Why is my real purpose for walking the camino?

Some Statistics: While we can never know the actual number of pilgrims on the caminos each year we do know from records kept at the Pilgrim Office _www.oficinadelperegrino.com_ that a total 347,578 pilgrims collected a Compostela in 2019 (pre Covid). Of these 40% gave a religious reason for their journey while 60% gave a spiritual or 'other' reasons for doing so. Contrary to popular belief the majority (54%) were between the ages of 30 and 60 and while there is a good gender balance women now outnumber men for the first time (51%). 94% arrived on foot, 5% arrived by bicycle, with the remaining: 406 by horseback, 243 by boat and 85 by wheelchair.

175 nations were represented last year, the majority: ❶ Spanish: 146,350 (42%) ❷ Italian 28,749 (8%) ❸ German 26,167 (7%) ❹ USA (20,652 (6%) ❺ Portugal 17,450 (5%) ❻ France 9,248 (2.7%) ❼ UK 9,132 (2.6%) ❽ Korea 8,224 (2.3%) ❾ Ireland 6,826 (2.0%) ❿ Brasil 6,025 (1.7%) ⓫ Australia 5,301 (1.5%) ⓬ Canada 5,279 (1.5%).

Pilgrims per month per camino

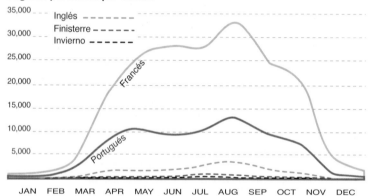

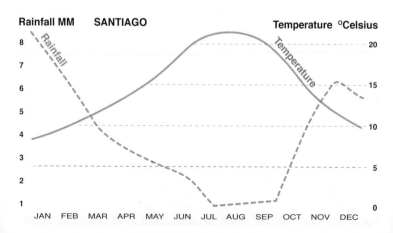

• **Abbreviations:** s/o = straight on / > turn right / < left / (right) on the right / c. = circa (about) / XIIc. = 12th century / adj. = adjacent or adjoining / incl. = inclusive / imm. = immediately / para. = parallel / €pp (per person). c/ = calle (street). r/ = rúa (road) / Av. = avenida (avenue) / ●*Alb.* = albergue (pilgrim hostal) / •*Apt.* = apartment / •*Hs* = hostal / €25-40 (single–double).

• **Map Legend:** Once you are familiar with the map symbols (Page 4) you should be able to easily find your way and identify places to stop and eat or sleep. Unlike conventional maps you always follow in the direction of the page so that everything appears sequentially on your left or right (similar to GPS systems such as Tom Tom). **Maps** show relevant information only and are therefore not strictly to scale – instead accurate distances are given between each facility or point of interest and corresponds to the text for ease of reference.

• **Text and place names** are shown as they appear 'on the ground' which is generally in Galician *Galego* but sometimes appear in Spanish *Castellano*. The Church of St. John may, therefore, appear as *Igrexa San Xoán* or *Igreja San Juan*. Villages in Galicia, tend to straggle without any defined centre and even the local church is frequently located outside the actual town. Distances are measured to a clearly defined feature.

• **Sun Compass:** this is provided on each map as an aid to orientation. Even in poor weather we can generally tell the direction of the sun. The general direction of these routes is westerly. Early in the morning the sun will be in the east and therefore 'behind' us and will gradually move around to appear over our left shoulder at midday. If you suddenly find yourself walking with the sun over your right shoulder – stop and make sure you are not following arrows *back* to your start point! In the evening the sun will be in our face so, likewise, if the

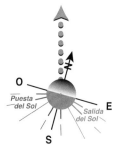

sun is behind you – stop and re-assess. You can also use this compass as an aid to understanding the human egoic tendency to identity ourselves as being at the centre of the universe. We say that the sun rises in the east *este* because that is our experience but of course it is the earth turning on its axis that turns us towards the sun in the morning and away from it at night. This is more than mere semantics – the very thought used to be a heresy punishable by death as Galileo was to discover. To understand why Finisterre is at the centre of the Santiago story we need to realise the vital importance of the sun and its orientation to ancient civilisations – not only its veneration as the source of life and regeneration with the rising sun *salida del sol* but its symbol of death and resurrection through the setting sun *puesta del sol* in the West *Oeste*.

• **Contour guides:** are shown for each stage. This provides an impression of the day's terrain and helps to prepare for the uphill stretches and anticipate the downhill ones. Contours are drawn to an exaggerated scale for emphasis.

• **Stages** *etapas:* Each stage is measured from the front door of one hostel to the next. Intermediate lodging is also shown, those directly on the route in a solid panel and those *off* with a border only (with distance). This way you can choose where to stay each night depending on your particular needs. **Adjusted distance:** In addition to *actual* distance a time equivalent is provided based on the cumulative ascent during each stage. This is based on the Naismith rule of adding 10 minutes for each 100m climbed.

Fitness Level	Speed	Time	20*km*	25*km*	30*km*	35*km*
			The distances (above) in kilometres will take the time (below) in hours			
Fast walker	5 kph	12 min /km	**4.0***hr*	**5.0***hr*	**6.0***hr*	**7.0***hr*
Average pace	4 kph	15 min /km	**5.0***hr*	**6.3***hr*	7.5hr	8.6*hr*
Leisurely pace	3 kph	20 min /km	**6.6***hr*	**8.3***hr*	—	—

As mentioned above these times need to be adjusted to allow for the ascent each day. For example **Stage 1** is **21.2** km but has a *cumulative* ascent of 650m or an 'extra' 65 minutes. An average pace walker would need to allow ±5hr 30 + 65 mins giving a total of 6 hrs 35 mins (a leisurely walker would need to allow ±8 hours 7 mins so should not consider more than a *maximum* of 25 km in any stage. We show the 'extra' time each day based on an average pace. •*Nota Bene!* Pace will *decrease,* often substantially, towards the end of a day. That is why pilgrims sometimes question the measurements given for the *last* section suggesting it was *double* the distance indicated (it took twice as long as expected). They were right about the time but not the distance! Take heed of the Chinese proverb, *'On a journey of a hundred miles, ninety is but half way'!*

• **Safety:** The camino offers a remarkably safe environment in an inherently unsafe world. When viewed in this context few cases of crime or harassment are reported but they have been known to occur. If you are a solo pilgrim and feel unsafe, keep other pilgrims in sight or ask to walk with someone until you feel comfortable again. Tim Cahill suggests, *'A journey is best measured in friends, rather than miles'.* In the event of an emergency or to report an incident the EU wide emergency number is 112. Road traffic is the major safety concern and extra vigilance is needed while on or crossing roadways.

• **Mobile Phones:** Recent years have seen an exponential rise in mobile phone use, impacting our individual and collective experience. The constant connectivity with our familiar *outer* world can keep us disconnected from the expansiveness of our *inner* world. This disconnect can diminish our relationship to each passing moment, the camaraderie of our 'camino family' and connection to our divine essence. Finding the courage to step outside our comfort zone can lead to Self-discovery. This may require limiting our dependency on external aids. While many of us may feel the need to carry a mobile phone for safety, orientation or other reasons perhaps we can, collectively, be more conscious about how and when we use them so as to minimise disturbance to other pilgrims... and ourSelves. See: *www.walkingtopresence.com.*

• **Pilgrim Passport** *Credencial***:** All Xunta hostels are reserved exclusively for pilgrims on the camino who must have a pilgrim passport *credencial* that has been stamped along the way. To apply for a **Compostela** you need to show your *credencial* stamped for at least 100km. A second stamp requirement was introduced in an effort to discourage those using interim transport. Stamps *sellos* are readily available from churches, hostels, even bars! *Credenciales* are readily available in Santiago or from your local confraternity which you are encouraged to join (see list of addresses p.95). To collect a **Fisterrana** or a **Muxiana** you need to have walked the entire way from Santiago.

• **Pilgrim hostels** *albergues de peregrinos* vary in what they provide but lodging is usually in bunk beds with additional overflow space on mattresses *colchonetas*. Number of beds and dormitories are shown in brackets *[8÷2] -v- [40÷1]* (simple division will provide an idea of density!) + private rooms *+4*. All Xunta and municipal hostels provide a kitchen with basic cooking equipment and a dining / sitting area. Opening times vary but most are cleaned and open again from early afternoon (13:00) to welcome pilgrims. Minicipal/Xunta albergues cannot be booked in advance and phone numbers are provided for emergency calls/to check availability outside the normal seasons (most are open all year but can close for holidays or maintenance purposes). *Note: Albergues are coming under new tourist regulations requiring additional facilities which is likely to raise the price of lodging.*

• **Costs:** Some monastery *convento Conv.* & parish *paroquia Par.* hostals ask for donations *donativo* and, unless we find ourselves destitute, we should leave at least €5 for a bed + €2 for basic breakfast and €8 for supper. Municipal hostals *Mun.* start at €6, Xunta *Xun.* €8. Private hostels *Priv.* €10-€17. This generally provides us with a bunk bed and use of a hot shower. Many offer additional facilities such as washing and drying machines for a small charge and many private hostals also provide individual rooms + from around €25. **Hotels** *•H*, hostales *•Hs*, pensiónes *•P* or casa rurales *•CR* literally 'rural house' (up-market B&B) vary widely from €30-€90 depending on season. Number of rooms (*x2* versus *x102*) indicates type (intimate -v- anonymous) and likely facilities on offer. Where a price range is shown in this guide the lower price is based on one person per night *individual* and the higher for 2 people sharing *doble*. Allow for a basic *minimum* €25 a day to include overnight stay at a Xunta hostel and remainder for food and drink. Some hostals provide a communal dinner (dependent on the warden *hospitalero*) and most have a basic kitchen *cocina* where a meal can be prepared. Alternatively most locations have one or more restaurants to choose from. Pilgrim menus *menú peregrino* are generally available for around €9 incl. wine. If you want to indulge in the wonderful seafood *mariscos* available in Galicia and accompany this with the delightful local *Albariño* wines expect to double or treble the basic cost!

Take time to **prepare a purpose for this pilgrimage** and consider completing the self-assessment questionnaire below. We might benefit by starting from the basis that we are essentially spiritual beings on a human journey. We came to learn some lesson and this pilgrimage affords an opportunity to find out what that is. Ask for help and expect it – it's there, now, waiting for us...

SELF-ASSESSMENT *INNER WAYMARKS These notes appear on a purple panel so you can easily skip over if they are of no interest or use to you.*

This self-assessment questionnaire is designed to encourage us to reflect on our life and its direction. We might view it as a snapshot of this moment in our evolving life-story. In the busyness that surrounds us we often fail to take stock of where we are headed. We are the authors of our unfolding drama and can re-write the script anytime we choose. Our next steps are up to us...

We might find it useful to initially answer these questions in quick succession as this may allow a more intuitive response. Afterwards, we can reflect more deeply and check if our intellectual response confirms these, change them or bring in other insights. Download copies of the questionnaire from the *Camino Guides* website – make extra copies so you can repeat the exercise on your return and again in (say) 6 months time. This way we can compare results and ensure we follow through on any insights and commitments that come to us while walking the camino.

❏ How do I differentiate pilgrimage from a long distance walk?
❏ How do I define spirituality – what does it mean to me?
❏ How is my spirituality expressed at home and at work?

❏ What do I see as the primary purpose of my life?
❏ Am I working consciously towards fulfilling that purpose?
❏ How clear am I on my goal and the right direction for me at this time?
❏ How will I recognise resistance to any changes required to reach my goal?

❏ When did I first become aware of a desire to take time-out?
❏ What prompted me originally to go on the camino de Santiago?
❏ Did the prompt come from something that I felt needed changing?
❏ Make a list of what appears to be blocking any change from happening.

❏ What help might I need on a practical, emotional and spiritual level?
❏ How will I recognise the right help or correct answer?
❏ What are the likely challenges in working towards my unique potential?
❏ What are my next steps towards fulfilling that potential?

How aware am I of the following? (score on a level of 1 – 10)
Compare these scores on returning from the camino... And again in, say, 6 months.

❏ Awareness of my inner spiritual world
❏ Clarity on what inspires me and the capacity to live my passion
❏ Confidence to follow my intuitive sense of the 'right' direction
❏ Ability to recognise the false egoic guide and the 'wrong' direction
❏ Ability to recognise my resistances and patterns of defence
❏ Ease with asking for, and receiving, support from others

REFLECTIONS:

"I am doing the camino once again, looking for something I left behind or perhaps never found. It's like coming home." Notes of a pilgrim from New Mexico. What are *my* reflections for this day?

_____
_____
_____
_____
_____
_____
_____
_____
_____
_____
_____
_____
_____
_____
_____

Going deeper? View www.inner-camino.com for guidance along the inner path.

Photo: **Monte Pindo** *the mythical Celtic abode of the gods 'Mount Olympus'.*

Centro Histórico: ❶ Convento de Santo Domingo de Bonaval XIIIth *(panteón de Castelao, Rosalía de Castro y museo do Pobo Galego)*. ❷ Mosteiro de San Martín Pinario XVIth *y museo* ❸ *Pazo de Xelmirez* XIIth ❹ Catedral XIIth –XVIIIth *Portica de Gloria, claustro, museo e tesouro* ❺ Hostal dos Reis Católicos XVth *Parador* ❻ Pazo de Raxoi XVIIIth *Presendencia da Xunta* ❼ Colexio de Fonseca XVIth *universidade y claustro* ❽ Capela y Fonte de Santiago ❾ Casa do Deán XVIIIth *Oficina do Peregrino (original)*. ❿ Casa Canónica *museo Peregrinaciónes*. ⓫ Mosteiro de San Paio de Antealtares XVth *Museo de Arte Sacra*. ⓬ S.Maria Salomé XIIth.

Santiago is a wonderful destination, full of vibrancy and colour. Pilgrims, musicians, tourists... all come and add to the life and soul of this fabled city. Stay awhile and visit her museums and markets. Soak up some of her culture or relax in the shaded *Alameda* park or stroll up the avenue of the Lions

Paseo dos Leónes to the statue of Rosalia de Castro and look out west over her belovéd Galicia and... *Finis terrae*.

TRAVEL to/from **Santiago:** *Check options with* <u>www.rome2rio.com</u>
See p. 54 for travel to/from **Finisterre** and p. 76 for travel to/from **Muxía**.
Monbus <u>www.monbus.com</u> run a daily service to Finisterre & Muxía stopping at villages along the way incl: Negreira-A Picota-Olveiroa-Dumbria-Cee.

AIR: *Direct flights to Santiago:* •*Easyjet* from London Gatwick, Geneva & Basle. •*Ryanair* from London Stansted, Frankfurt & Milan. •*Vueling* from London, Paris, Brussels, Amsterdam & Zurich. •*Aer Lingus* from Dublin (summer schedule). •*BA / Iberia* and other major airlines offer regular services throughout the year via various connecting airports in Spain, mainly Madrid. *Vueling* also direct from London to *A Coruña* and *Asturias*. Check other possibilities from / to nearby airports at A Coruña, Vigo, Porto – all of which have regular rail and bus connections to/from Santiago. Owing to ongoing Covid restrictions, all schedules may change at short notice. Due to the increasing impact of aviation on climate change consider:

BUS: book online (paypal only) with **ALSA** <u>alsa.com</u> direct services to Santiago from Madrid airport and other major cities within Spain.

RAIL: book online through Spanish rail network **RENFE** <u>renfe.com</u> or **RAIL EUROPE** <u>raileurope.co.uk</u> direct services to Santiago from Madrid *Chamartin* and other major cities within Spain.

FERRY: Travelling by sea provides a chance to acclimatise slowly and reduce our carbon footprint. Check Brittany Ferries: Portsmouth & Plymouth to Santander <u>brittany-ferries.co.uk</u> with onward travel to Santiago by bus or rail.

Muxianna

Credencial del Peregrino

Fisterrana

In addition to the Compostela a Fisterana and Muxiana are available to all pilgrims walking to either Muxia or Finisterre. In each case proof of walking is required by having the *credencial* stamped along the way.

❶ Turismo *Centro*: r/ Vilar 63 © 981 555 129 _www.santiagoturismo.com_ *May-Oct: 09:00-19.00 (winter 17:00)* ● **Tur Galicia** Praza de Mazarelos 10:00 / 17:00 ● **Pilgrim Services** Rúa Nova 7 (adj. catedral) © 912 913 756 left luggage €3. ●**Laundromat SC18** 09:00-22:00 Rúa San Clemente 18.

● *Albergues:* **€10-€20** *(depending on season / beds per dormitory)* ❶–❾ *(camino Francés)*. ▌ **Rúa Concheiros Nº48** *(see map>)* ❿ **El Viejo Quijote** *Priv.[20÷2]* © 881 088 789. **Nº36** ⓫ **La Estrella** *Priv.[24÷6]* © 617 882 529. **Nº10** ⓬ **Porta Real** *Priv.[20÷6]* © 633 610 114. ▌ **Belvís**  **+500m** ⓭ **Seminario Menor** *Conv.[173÷12]+81* © 881 031 768 _www.alberguesdelcamino.com_ Av. Quiroga Palacios *(see photo above)*. ▌ **c/ S.Clara** ⓮ **La Salle** *Priv.[84÷14]* © 981 585 667 ▌ **c/ Basquiños Nº45** ⓯ **Basquiños** *Priv.[8÷1]* © 661 894 536 **Nº67** ⓰ **Meiga Backpackers** *Priv.[28÷5]* © 981 570 846.

● **Centro Histórico:** ⓱ **O Fogar de Teodomiro** *Priv.[20÷5]+* © 981 582 920 Plaza de Algalia de Arriba 3. ⓲ **The Last Stamp** *Priv.[62÷10]* © 981 563 525 r/ Preguntorio 10. ⓳ **Azabache** *Priv.[20÷5]* © 981 071 254 c/Azabachería 15. ⓴ **Km.0** *Priv.[50÷10]* (€ 18-26) © 881 974 992 _www.santiagokm0.es_ r/ Carretas 11 (new renovation by pilgrim office) ㉑ **Blanco** *Priv.[20÷2]+ +€35-55* © 881 976 850 r/ Galeras 30. ㉒ **Mundoalbergue** *Priv.[34÷1]* © 981 588 625 c/ San Clemente 26. ㉓ *Roots & Boots (closed temp.)* Priv.[48÷6]© 699 631 594 r/Campo Cruceiro do Galo. ● *Otros:* ㉔ **La Estación** *Priv.[24÷2]* © 981 594 624 r/ Xoana Nogueira 14 (adj. rail station **+2.9** km). ㉕ **Compostela Inn** *Priv.[120÷30]+* © 981 819 030 off *AC-841 (adj. H Congreso +6.0 km)*.

● *Hoteles* **€30–60:** •Hs **Santiago** © 608 865 895 r/Senra 11. •Hs **Moure** © 981 583 637 r/dos Loureiros. •H **Fonte S. Roque** © 981 554 447 r/do Hospitallilo 8. •Hs **Estrela** © 981 576 924 Plaza de San Martín Pinario 5. •Hs **San Martín Pinario** *x127* © 981 560 282 _www.hsanmartinpinario.com_ Praza da Inmaculada. •**Pico Sacro** r/San Francisco 22 © 981 584 466. •H** **Montes** © 981 574 458 _www.hotelmontes.es_ r/ Raíña 11. **Rúa Fonseca Nº1** •P **Fonseca** © 603 259 337. **Nº5** •Hs **Libredon** 981 576 520 & •P **Barbantes / Celsa** ©981 583 271 on r/ Franco 3. **Rúa Vilar Nº8** •H**Rua Vilar** © 981 519 858. **Nº17** •H**Airas Nunes** © 981 569 350. **Nº65** •Hs**Suso** © 981 586 611 _www.hostalsuso.com_. **Nº76** •Hs **Santo Grial** © 629 515 961. •**A Nosa Casa** © 981 585 926 r/ Entremuralles 9 adj. •Hs **Mapoula** © 981 580 124. •Hs **Alameda** © 981 588 100 San Clemente 32. ● *€60–90:* •H **A Casa Peregrino** © 981 573 931 c/ Azabachería. •**Entrecercas** © 981 571 151 r/Entrecercas. **Porta de Pena Nº17** •H **Costa Vella** © 981 569 530 (+ Jardín) **Nº5** •P **Casa Felisa** © 981 582 602 (+Jardín). •**MV Algalia** © 981 558 111 Praza Algalia de Arriba 5. •H***Pazo De Altamira** © 981 558 542 r/ Altamira, 18. ● *€100+* •H*** **San Francisco** Campillo de San Francisco © 981 581 634. •H*** **Hostal de los Reyes Católicos** Plaza Obradoiro © 981 582 200.

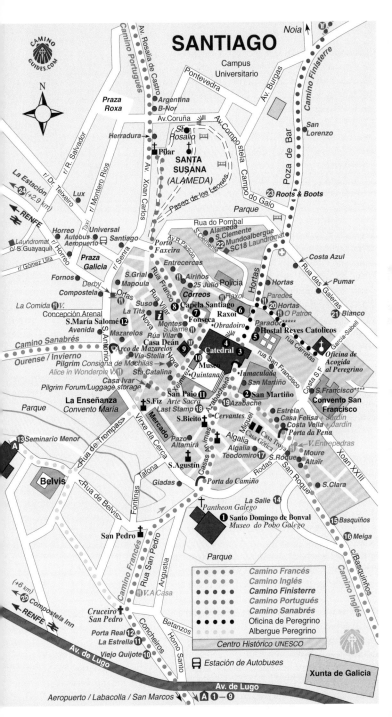

Santiago Cathedral 4 squares *prazas*:

■ **Praza do Obradoiro**. The 'golden' square of Santiago is usually thronged with pilgrims and tourists admiring the dramatic west facing façade of the Cathedral, universal symbol of Santiago, with St. James looking down on all the activity from his niche in the central tower. This provides the main entrance to the Cathedral and the Portico de Gloria. To the right of the steps is the discrete entrance to the museum. A combined ticket will provide access to all rooms including the crypt and the cloisters and also to the 12th century palace of one of Santiago's most famous individuals and first archbishop, Gelmírez *Pazo de Xelmírez* situated on the (left). In this square we also find the beautiful Renaissance façade of the Parador named after Ferdinand and Isabel *Hostal dos Reis Católicos* on whose orders it was built in 1492 as a pilgrim hospice. Opposite the Cathedral is the more austere neoclassical seat of the Galician government and town hall *Pazo de Raxoi* with its solid arcade. Finally, making up the fourth side of the square is the gable end of the *Colegio de S. Jerónimo* part of the university. Moving anti-clockwise around the cathedral – turn up into Rúa de Fonseca to:

■ **Praza das Praterías**. The most intimate of the squares with its lovely centrepiece, an ornate statue of horses leaping out of the water. On the corner of Rúa do Vilar we find the Dean's House *Casa do Deán* formerly the pilgrim office. Along the walls of the Cathedral itself are the silversmith's *plateros* that give the square its name. Up the steep flight of steps we come to the magnificent southern door to the Cathedral, the oldest extant doorway and traditionally the entrance taken by pilgrims coming from Portugal. The quality of the carvings and their arrangement is remarkable and amongst the many sculptured figures is one of St. James between two cypress trees. Continuing around to the left we come to:

■ **Praza da Quintana.** This wide square is identified by the broad sweep of steps separating the lower part *Quintana of the dead* from the upper *Quintana of the living*. Opp the Cathedral is the wall of the *Mosteiro de San Paio de Antealtares* (with museum of sacred art). The square provides the eastern entrance to the Cathedral via the Holy Gate *Porta Santa* sometime referred to as the Door of Pardon *El Perdón* only opened during Holy Years. The next (after 2021) will be . Adjoining it is the main entrance to the Cathedral shop that has several guidebooks (in various languages) with details of the Cathedral's many chapels and their interesting carvings and statuary and the priceless artefacts and treasures in the museum. Finally, we head up the broad flight of steps around the corner and back into:

■ **Praza da Inmaculada (Azabachería)** to the north facing Azabachería façade, with the least well-known doorway and the only one that *descends* to enter the Cathedral. It has the most weathered aspect, with moss and lichen covering its bleak exterior. Opposite the cathedral is the imposing southern edifice of *Mosteiro de San Martiño Pinario* the square in front gets any available sun and attracts street artists. The archbishop's arch *Arco Arzobispal* brings us back to the Praza do Obradoiro.

❶ The **Pilgrim Office** *Oficina del Peregrino* now at Rua Carretas *below the parador* Ⓒ 981 568 846 open daily 09:00-21:00 (10:00-20:00 winter). The new office has tight security procedure (expect lengthy delays). It lacks the informal atmosphere of the former office in Rua Vilar with its team of friendly *Amigos*. However, providing you have fulfilled the criteria of a bona fide pilgrim and walked back from Finisterre via Muxia for religious/spiritual reasons and collected 2 stamps per day on your *credencial* you will have completed the minimum 100 km requirement and can apply for a *Compostela*

which may entitle you to certain privileges such as reduced entry fees to museums and a free meal at the Parador! If you do not fulfil the criteria you can still obtain a **certificado** (€3) which is essentially a certificate of distance travelled. The welcoming Companions meet in a room behind the adjoining pilgrim chapel (see below).

•**Camino Companions** meet in the pilgrim office room 6 first floor (Mon-Sat) 11:30 & 15:00 for mindful reflection. Daily mass in English in the pilgrim chapel 09:30 check for updates at: *www.facebook.com/CaminoCompanions*
•**The Camino Chaplaincy** Church of England – All welcome Ⓒ 698 128 190 with services in English daily May–Oct. Check times & chapel on *www. facebook.com/CaminoChaplaincyCoE/* or with *www.egeria.house/updates/*
•**Pilgrim House** rua Nova 19 also offers a place of welcome and reflection daily 10.00–14:00 (closed Wed & Sun) Ⓒ 981 585 788 under the care of Terra Nova USA *www.pilgrimhousesantiago.com*

1 SANTIAGO – NEGREIRA – 21.2 km

⬚⬚⬚⬚⬚	--- ---	6.8 --- ---	32%
▬▬▬	--- ---	13.4 --- ---	63%
▬▬▬	--- ---	1.0 --- ---	5%
Total km		**21.2 km** *(13.2 ml)*	

▲ Total Ascent 650m +65 mins*
Alto.m ▲ Mar do Ovellas **285**m *(935 ft)*
< Ⓐ Ⓗ > ➲*Quintáns* **7.1** km +*Roxos 0.8km*
➲Lombao **10.5** km +*0.5km* ➲ Chancela **20.5** ➲*Logroso +0.7km*

The Practical Path: This first stage out of Santiago is the shortest but be prepared for the very steep climb from Augapesada up to Trasmonte (*Allow ±5½ hours to walk 21.2 km at average pace of 4 kph [21.2÷4] +65 mins for cumulative ascent of 650m ± 6½ hours total. See p18).* Stay alert for old waymarks that may direct us back onto the busy C-543. Recent work by the *Amigos* has increased natural pathways to a third much of it through eucalyptus and pine forest which offers shade from the sun or shelter from the rain. Drinking fonts are few and far between – fill your flask before leaving Santiago.

The Mystical Path: We walk by faith, not by sight. *Corinthians 5:7.* We are surrounded by trivia. There is much to distract us from the inner path, but what profit is there in the outward journey if it is not accompanied by expanded awareness? A pilgrim must travel on two paths simultaneously. The tourist will look for the stone altar, the pilgrim an altered state. The one seeks sacred sites the other insight. Will we make time today for contemplation and reflection?

The Bible in Spain: "... I have always found in the disposition of the children of the fields a more determined tendency to religion and piety than amongst the inhabitants of the towns and cities, and the reason is obvious – they are less acquainted with the works of man's hands than those of God... the scoffers at religion do not spring from amongst the simple children of nature, but are the excrescences of over-wrought refinement." *George Borrow*

0.0 km **Leave the cathedral** by the main (west) entrance and take the access road down past the Parador and police station and Igrexa de San Fructuoso. Continue s/o along rúa das Hortas and over the busy intersection (✿*Farmacia* right) at **Campo das Hortas [0.4** km] into rúa Poza do Bar (Alb. Roots & Boots left) pass •H¨*San Lorenzo* to park of ancient oak trees at **Carballeira de San Lorenzo [0.6** km]

CAMINO
GUIDES.COM

[+0.9 km] *Xunta* **8** A
Centro **0.7** ← **7**
NEGREIRA (Pop. 7,000)

© *Casa da Bola*

3 ← **3.4** **Chancela Anjana**

[+0.8 km] *Logroso* **2** A
Logroso

Cruce

1 A *Bergando* [+0.9 km]

Barquiña

Ponte Nova

† *Capilla S. Blas*

río Tambre

← **1.8** **Ponte Maceira**

Ponte Maceira

Burguieros

Reino

Pancho

3.5 **Trasmonte**

▲ *Alto Mar do Ovellas 285m*

Carballo

F *Fonte Sta. Maria*

Castelo de Altamira

Pedrouzos

Portanxil

(Brión)

fútbol

Dos Pasos

Carmen

2.8 **Augapesada**

Puente

O Cruceiro

A *Casa Riamonte* [+0.5 km]

Bertamirans
(Ames)

Monte da Costa
232m
▲ *Alto do Vento*

Lombao

Ventosa

Ames

Alto do Vento **1.9**

río Roxos

Piñor

3.1 **Quintáns**

El Asador
Roxos
[+0.7 km] *O Desvío* A

A

Os Arcos

Carballal (Vilestro)

río Fontecova

3.0 **Puente**

Vidan

río Sar

Monte Pedroso
(460m)

Sarela de Abaixo

Puente
río Sarela

Universitario

1.0 **Parque** *San Lorenzo*

Alameda

SANTIAGO
(Pop. 90,000)

† H *Parador*

0.0 **Catedral**

1.0 km **Parque** *San Lorenzo* Adj. the park is Convento de San Lorenzo de Trasouto *XIII*. *[An alternative route from the Cathedral via the Parque de Santa Susanna joins from the left].* The small park offers shaded seating and fountain. We now have a tranquil 3 km of path through woodland. Waymarks take us down a steep concrete road to a stone bridge over the **Río Sarela [0.4 km]** veer <left over the river onto path alongside derelict mill across small stream to climb up through mixed woodland where the path rejoins a quiet road in the small hamlet of **Sarela de Abaixo [0.7 km]**. Here we can take a last look back to the spires of the cathedral and the city of Santiago. Turn down <left past the row of new houses and turn up right> (**past Nº 53**) **[0.2 km]** and take path through the Eucalyptus forest on a rough walled lane to the top of a rise. The path now descends to rejoin asphalt road down to bridge over the **Río Fontecova [1.7 km]**

3.0 km **Puente** *Río Fontecova (tributary of the río Sar).* Keep s/o up steeply veering right> to T-junction and turn down <left into **Carballal** (parish of Vilestro) veer right> by bus-stop at village signboard and horreo. Continue out of the village and down to cross small stream and turn up steeply right> by high orchard wall onto woodland path crossing several local roads and up to village crossroads at:

3.1 km **Quintáns** ☕ *Bar Os Arcos (right)* turn <left & imm. right> by bus shelter. ▲ *[Detour Roxos: 0.7 km. •H¨O Desvío x20 €60-70 © 981 815 994 www.hotelodesvio.com + •H¨El Asador de Roxos x8 €50+ © 981 815 973 Directions: From bus shelter keep s/o down through suburbs to roundabout in Roxos on C-543].* At bus shelter turn down steeply turn right> at T-junction to **Puente Río Roxos [0.6 km]** with picnic tables in shaded glade adj. bridge over the river. The road takes us through **Portela** where the path then turns right> into woodland to emerge onto the **main road [1.3 km]** at:

1.9 km **Alto do Vento** popular ☕ *Alto do Vento.* Here we pass into the Concello de Ames and continue down the main road AC-453 veering right> through the village of **Ventosa** and over [!] main road onto track and back to main road up to crossroads at **Lombao [1.5 km]**. ▲ *[Detour Castelo: 0.6 km. •Casa Riamonte Priv. [4÷1] €14 +4 €45 check if open) © 981 890 356].* From Lombao continue s/o passing ☕ O Cruceiro **[0.8 km]** adj. ✚*Farmacia* turni <left to medieval footbridge in Augapesada and back up to road **[0.5 km]**:

2.8 km **Augapesada** Keep s/o over road *[☕ Bar/shop* Carmen *50m left]* onto concrete path. From here it's a steep uphill climb for 2.8 km through pine and eucalyptus forest. The track emerges onto the main road by radio mast. Continue past wayside fountain and picnic area *[☼ fonte Santa Maria Trasmonte* shortly afterwards we reach the high point ▲ 285m *Alto do Mar de Ovellas* and then down through the hamlet of **Carballo** into **Trasmonte**.

3.5 km **Trasmonte** crossroads hamlet with ☕ *Bar* Casa Pancho. Cruceiro of St. James and Parish church of Santa Maria with baroque tower just off route on the road to the left. ▲ *[Detour Castelo de Altamira: A 4 km round trip by road via Portanxil, Leboráns to A Torre above Brións. The route is* **Not** *waymarked].* From Trasmonte it's all the way downhill through the small hamlets of: **Reino** (note sign left for *mesón O Pozo 80m is in fact 300m down steeply to main road!*). **Burgueiros** and finally Ponte Maceira.

1.8 km **Ponte Maceira** ⅋ *Ponte Maceira* overlooking the río Tambre, weir and magnificent medieval bridge (restored). A delightful place to rest and, perhaps, bathe the feet in the cool waters. The hamlet is one of the best-preserved in Galicia with fine mansions *pazos* with armorial shields lining the river bank. *[In a legend, reminiscent of the Red Sea biblical story, we are told that God destroyed the bridge in a single stroke to prevent Roman soldiers based at Dugium (Duio in Fisterra) pursuing the cortège of St. James].* This enduring myth lives on in the coat of arms of the local council. A reflection, perhaps, of the continuing split between the authority of church and state and between inner and outer authority. As Ralph Waldo Emerson reminds us in *Essays of the Over-Soul*, 'The faith that stands on authority is not faith.'

Concello de Negreira

Ponte Maceira

Once over the river you enter the **Concello de Negreira**. Turn <left over the bridge passing the Capilla de San Blas and wayside cross *cruceiro* (left) and *[⚱]* *non drinkable* (right). Veer <left onto track through oak woods alongside river under arch of road bridge *Puente Nuevo*. The path meanders through crop fields to rejoin the road by car showrooms in **Outeiros**. Continue through **Barca** and turn up <left at next junction (signposted A Chancela / Logrosa) to 14thC Pazo Albariña (left).

[Here legend tells of the lord of this Manor House who left his son in the care of a nurse while he went on a crusade against the Moors. When he returned he learnt that his son had drowned in the waters of the Río Tambre. He demanded the nurse be beheaded and at the moment the axe fell her husband also knelt with her and both were decapitated together. They were buried amongst the pines trees and it is said that the sighing of the pines here reflects their last embrace. This story is also reminiscent of the theme in the Galician anthem The Pines Os Pinos that calls on Galicians to listen to the murmuring pines which is none other than the voice of the ancestors calling on the people to throw off the yoke of oppression and servitude.

3.4 km Chancela de Abaixo *Options.* We have several options at this point.

[Detour Ⓐ Monte Bergando 0.9 km: Alb.❶ *Bergando* Priv.*[28÷1] €15 +5 €50 Rocio ©* 981 521 357. **Directions:** *Turn right up rua Chancela over AC-447 & the town bypass AC-544 onto Av. Santiago (in reality a small country lane through woodland) to this peaceful rural location].*

[Detour Ⓑ Logrosa 0.7 km: Alb.❷ *Logrosa* Priv.*[20÷2] €17 +6 €30-€40* ©981 885 820 (m: 646 142 554 Antonio y Luis). **Directions:** *Turn down opp. Alb. Anjana & continue for 800m past church to albergue (signposted right). Welcoming hostel and quiet garden. Dinner available.*

[Detour Ⓒ Take lane (right) imm. *after* Alb. Anjana to go direct to •*H¨Millan* (prev. *Tamara) x60* €30-50 © 981 885 201 *www.hotelmillan.es* Av. Santiago. Behind the hotel is a short-cut through woodland to *Alb.* ❺ **San José** Priv. *[50÷3]* €14 *+15* €25-35) © 881 976 934 *www.alberguesanjose.es* Rúa de Castelao 400m from town centre].

From Chancela (Pazo Albariña) keep s/o past *Alb.*❸ *Anjana* Priv.*[20÷3]* €14 with bar and terrace © 607 387 229 Lugar Chancela 39. *[Note: the municipal hostel is still 1.6 km (1.0 km on the far side of the town centre). Rejoin main road into* **Negreira**. Pilgrim information kiosk (summer) and 50m (right) *Alb.* ❹ **Alecrin** Priv.*[40÷2]* €14 © 981 818 286 Av. Santiago 52 *(Hotel Millán beyond).* For town centre turn <left over Rio de Duomes (tributary of río Tambre). Proceed up Av. de Santiago past Nº22 *Alb.* ❻ **Lua** Priv. *[40÷1]* €14 © 698 128 883 modern building (left). *[Opp. Alb. Lua is alt. access road to albergue San José].* Pass modern statues of medieval pilgrim to:

0.7 km Negreira *centro* crossroads *Alb.* ❼ **Carmen** Priv.*[30÷2]* €14 ©981 881 652 [m] 636 129 691 (Mari Carmen) c/Carmen 2 part of •*Hs/*❙ **La Mezquito** *x7* €30-50 (same owner). opp. 🍴 *Gadis* supermarket 9:30a.m. – 9:30 p.m. •*CR* **Casa Néboa** *x10* €60-70 © 680 335 new upmarket offering in traditional style stone building with its own bar and

restaurant on Calle Vilachán de Arriba, 5 (300m from statue of Emigrante).

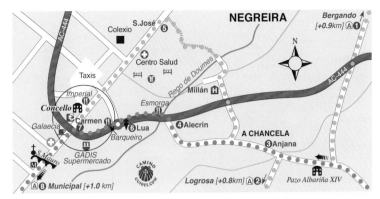

The Municipal albergue is located a further 1.0 km out of town (see photo>) *Alb.* **❽ Municipal** *Xunta. [22÷2]* €8 © 664 081 498 additional space in tents in summer season. Modern purpose-built building with good shower & toilet facilities and kitchenette (buy food before arriving). Directions: (see next stage).

Negreira population 7,000 with variety of shops, bank ATM's and local council office *Concello de Negreira* © 981 885 550. Taxi rank © 981 885 515 / also Taxi Ramón © 626 033 879 centrally located off c/ Carmen. Several bars and restaurants incl. the popular ¶ *Imperial* on c/Carmen with terrace to the rear where Pilar and English husband Davíd may still provide home cooking from 12:00 onwards or try the central ¶ *Barqueiro* on Av. Santiago. 🍴 *Cervecería Galaecia* on corner of c/San Mauro serves breakfast from 6:30 a.m. and further down the street is 🍴 *Rios* (by statue see below) and 🍴 *Bar Porto* with terrace over the river. Negreira's relative modernity belies its early foundations. The coat of arms of the local council portrays the destruction of the bridge over the Río Tambre (see legend and photo previous page).

Just below the arch is a delightful shaded square with benches and fountain and here we find a masterpiece in evocative sculpture of an émigré leaving his family to seek work in the brave New World *Monumento al emigrante*. It reflects the constant emigration, particularly of men, from Galicia down through the ages.

The illustrious Counts of Altamira, whose power in the 15th century extended over the whole of this area to the walls of Santiago city itself, occupied the manor house **Pazo do Cotón** and adj. **Capela de San Mauro** that we pass at the start of stage 2. Their main seat was Castelo Altamira now in ruins *[located off the camino 2 km from Trasmonte]*.

Note: The next stage is the longest at 33.8 kilometres and you will need to start early if you intend to reach Olveiroa by evening. However several new albergues provide intermediate lodging and there is a free pick-up & drop-off service next day from As Maroñas / Santa Mariña to the following *off* route hotels: *A Picota* (+2.5 km) – Santa Baia (+11 km) – *Santa Comba* (+12 km) and Outes (+14 km). Shop for food or energy snacks before the shops close on the night before.

REFLECTIONS:

_____
_____
_____
_____
_____
_____
_____
_____
_____
_____
_____
_____
_____
_____
_____
_____
_____
_____
_____
_____
_____
_____
_____
_____
_____
_____
_____
_____
_____
_____
_____
_____
_____
_____

Praza y Pozo do Cotón *Monumento al emigrante & Capela San Mauro*

2 NEGREIRA – OLVEIROA

⋯⋯⋯	--- ---	11.0	--- --- 33%
▬▬▬	--- ---	22.3	--- --- 66%
▬▬▬	--- ---	0.5	--- --- 1%
Total km		**33.8** km (21.0 ml)	

Total Ascent 630m ± **63** *mins*
*Alto.*m ▲ Monte Aro **420**m *(1,380 ft)*
< **A** **H** > ➲Vilaserío **13.0** km ➲Maroñas /S.Mariña **21.0** ➲Lago **28.0** km
➲*A Picota* **28.4** *(+2.9km)* ➲Mallon / Ponte Olveira **31.7** km

The Practical Path: While Olveiroa has excellent facilities this is a long stage with 66% on road *(time on asphalt can be reduced by taking the 'green' routes)*. However, there is interim lodging **Maroñas** at **21.0** km. **Lago** is around midway between Negreira and Cee at **27.6** km leaving **25.3** km to **Cee** and **12.1** km to **Finisterre** making a more leisurely 4 stages in total. Several hotels provide a free pick-up service from Maroñas and Lago which alleviates pressure on lodging. Buy energy snacks in Negreira and fill up water bottles.

The Mystical Path: *As a well-spent day brings happy sleep, so life well used brings happy death. Leonardo da Vinci.* We generally experience death and dying as unwelcome visitors. Yet to be born anew we must first allow our old out-worn perceptions die. Over-identification with our physical bodies limits our understanding of Who we are and induces fear and a sense of vulnerability. We need to let go of outworn beliefs if we want to become part of the New.

Personal Notes: *"... with what little strength remained I hung my sodden clothes above the fire and raked the dying embers. As I stumbled up the stairs my candle blew out with the gale-force wind that howled through the broken window. I relit it and in the brief moment before it was again extinguished I caught the surreal reflection of numerous dolls scattered over the floor. I was aware that I was alone but the fear of loneliness died in me that night. Exhaustion flooded over me and sweet sleep came to drown out the noise of the storm outside..."*

0.0 km **Leaving the centre of Negreira** *[Alb.❼ Carmen Mezquito crossroads]* head down calle San Mauro under the stone archway (emigrant statue right) to bridge over **Río Barcala [0.5 km]** and optional river route right (see next page). For main route keep s/o and veer <left at fork up to sign

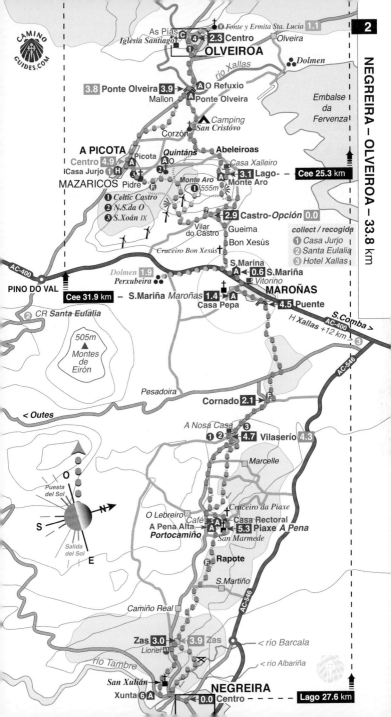

CAMINO GUIDES.COM

✠ *Fonte y Ermita Sta. Lucia* **1.1**

As Pías
Iglesia Santiago **4** ← **2.3** Centro
OLVEIROA   *Olveira*

1

Dolmen

rio Xallas

Embalse
da
Fervenza

3.8 Ponte Olveira **3.9**   **A** O *Refuxio*
Mallon   **A** ← Ponte Olveira

▲ *Camping*
✠ *San Cristóvo*
Corzón

A PICOTA   *Quintáns*
Centro **4.9**   **A** O
I*Casa Jurjo* **1** **H**   *Picota* **2**   *Abeleiras*
MAZARICOS ✠ *Pidre*   **3**   **F**   *Casa Xalleiro*
1 *Celtic Castro*   *Monte Aro*   **3.1** Lago-   — **Cee 25.3 km**
2 *N.S.da O*   **1** *555m*   Monte Aro
3 *S.Xoán IX*   **2.9** Castro-*Opción* **0.0**

Vilar
do Castro   *Gueima*
Bon Xesús   *collect / recogida*
Cruceiro Bon Xesús ✠   **1** *Casa Jurjo*
2 *Santa Eulalia*
3 *Hotel Xallas*

AC-400

PINO DO VAL   *Dolmen* **1.9**   S.Marina
Perxubeira   **A** ← **0.6** S.Mariña
Vitorino
Cee 31.9 km – S.Mariña *Maroñas* **1.4**   **MAROÑAS**
2 *CR Santa Eulalia*   ✠   **S.Comba >**
Casa Pepa   **← 4.5** Puente
H Xallas +12 km   **AC-400**

505m
▲
Montes
de Eirón
Pesadoira

AC-546

< Outes

Cornado **2.1**   **F**

O
Puesta
del Sol
A Nosa Casa
1 **2** **3** ← **4.7** Vilaserío **4.3**
S
Marcelle
Salida
del Sol
E

Cruceiro da Piaxe ✠
O Lebreiro *Café*   **A** **Casa Rectoral**
A Pena Alta ← **A** ← **5.3** Piaxe *A Pena*
Portocamiño   **A**
San Marmede

F
Rapote
S.Martiño

Camiño Real

Zas **3.0** ← **3.9** Zas
Lionel □   **< rio Barcala**
rio Tambre   **< rio Albariña**

San Xulián ✠
Xunta **6** **A**   **NEGREIRA**
Xunta ← **0.0** Centro – – – **Lago 27.6 km**

for Negreira **Iglesia [0.2 km]** *[Alb.❾ Municipal Xunta s/o left 200m].* Turn off right> and head up past church of **San Xulián** *XVI* up steps onto laneway veering <left onto woodland path. Continue s/o up Alto da Cruz to rejoin the asphalt road into **Zas [2.3 km]:**

3.0 km **Zas** Turn right> opp. shop *Lionel* where the alt. river route joins.

●●●● *Alternative River Route Bonita Alternativa! recommended* ✔ *3.9 km –v– 3.0 km.* Turn right over bridge and follow the delightful *río Barcala* upstream passing cascades (photo>) and cross access road to picnic site & **Park [2.4 km]** *Aula da Natureza* before crossing back onto woodland paths that climb up steeply to rejoin main route in **Zas [1.5 km].**

The camino continues via **Zas** onto peaceful woodland paths up through eucalyptus and oak woods that skirt around **Camiño Real** crossing a quiet country lane *[to San Martiño]* past rest area in **Rapote [3.9 km]** [⛲] *fonte de Rapote* into **A Pena [1.4 km].**

5.3 km **A Pena** *Piaxe* Igrexa San Mamede •*CR*+ •*Alb.* **Rectoral S. Mamede da Pena** *Priv.[22÷3]* €15 +5 €35-60 ℂ 649 948 014 links at rear to 🛏 & •*Alb.* **Alto da Pena** *Priv.[20÷6]* €15 +2 €50 Portocamiño (Manuel y Jennifer) ℂ 609 853 486. Keep s/o to crossroads at **A Pena / Piaxe [0.3 km]** past ancient stone crossroads *cruceiro*

and turn right on main road [!] *(Portocamiño left)* past sign for *Parque Ecólico de Corzón [part of the extensive wind turbine infrastructure of Galicia]* and veer right off road to junction of earth tracks by sign for Lebreiro and **option** ■ **[0.9 km].** (see below for alternative route to Vilaserío). For main route keep s/o left (farm building on right) up track that winds its way back to the **main road** [!] **[1.0 km].** Stay on the CP-5603 and watch out for turn off <**left [2.1 km]** [!] ('70 kph' sign) onto path passing small pilgrims shop *Casa da Sabia* then down to **Vilaserío [0.4 km].**

●●●● *Alternative Route by earth track (recommended* ✔*): 4.3 km –v– 4.4 km.* Continue s/o right at **option** ■ past farm building (left) and continue along contour line onto pleasant farm track parallel to main road now above to our left. This continues over cross tracks with sign for Vilaserío sharp left to rejoin main route by *Casa da Sabia* and down into Vilaserío.

4.7 km **Vilaserío** *Alb.*❶ **O Rueiro** *Priv.[30÷3]* €12 +6 €35 ℂ 981 893

561 (in trad. village house) adj. popular 🍴 Herminio / A Nosa Casa *Alb.* ❷ **Casa Vella** *Priv.[14÷1]* €12 *+3* €35-50 Ⓒ 981 893 516 (José y Visi) menú. Continue on main road to old **schoolhouse [0.5** km] *Alb.* ❸ **Escuela** *Muni. [14÷1]* € donation Ⓒ 648 792 029 (key with Nidia house Nº 39 blue façade opp). Basic hostel. Continue on main road to turn-off right> into **Cornado [1.6** km]:

2.1 km **Cornado** [⛲] fonte *Cornada [Remains of the largest Roman garrison in Galicia, dating from in the first century, have recently been discovered in the area]*. Turn up <left at the fonte onto forest track right> on main road and <left back onto farm tracks into **Maroñas [4.5** km]:

4.5 km **As Maroñas** *Puente* s/o over bridge *río Maroñas* (good picnic spot) and into *Concello de Mazaricos*. Turn <left at crossroads and <left again at T-Junction [Note: right As Maroñas with panadería on main road and pick-up for hotel Xallas].

1.4 km **Santa Mariña** *As Maroñas* 50m left cruceiro and ●*Alb.*Casa Pepa *Priv.[38÷5]* €14 *+6* €45-50 Ⓒ 981 852 881 (Flora y Paco) popular bar (see photo>). ■ *Note: if hostels in the area are full or there is not sufficient time to reach Lago/Olveiroa contact the following off-route hotels and/or take a taxi. Casa Jurjo offers a free and reliable pick-up and*

drop-off service for pilgrims (or walk the newly waymarked route over Monte Aro via alt. green route direct to A Picota –see next page).

❶ *H* **Casa Jurjo** €40-50 Ⓒ 981 852 015 *A Picota* +2.9 km (free pick-up)
❷ *H* **Santa Eulalia** €40+ Ⓒ 981 877 262 *Santa Baia* +11 km (taxi)
❸ *H* **Xallas** €35-46 Ⓒ 981 880 708 *Santa Comba* +12 km (taxi)

To continue turn right at wayside cross past picnic area (left) and <left on main road (LC-403) passing 🍴 Casa Vitoriano to 🍴 *bar Gallego* / Antelo and adj. albergue:

0.6 km **Santa Mariña** *LC-403* ●*Alb.* **Santa Mariña** *Priv.[32÷3]* €12 Ⓒ 981 852 897 m: 655 806 800 stone building directly on main road with additional beds in new extension under café Gallego – alt. pick-up point *recogida* for off-route hotels. From albergue continue to junction **right>** [**0.3** km] signposted Bon Xesus [*Detour: s/o to Dolmen Perxubeira see p.42]*. Monte Aro is now visible ahead as we pass wayside cross (left) through hamlet of **Bon Xesus [1.5** km] *[site of a medieval pilgrim hospital]* and **Xeima** and up to camino option and **signboard [1.1** km].

2.9 km **Castro** *Option* ▲ [?] Turn right> at signboard for main route.

Alternative via A Picota ● ● ● ● *8.7 km –v– 7.2 km.* This route is now well waymarked with green arrows on traditional *mojón* marked *camiño verde / camiño complentario – A Picota.* ▲ Turn <left at **signboard [0.0 km]** and up **right>** [0.3 km] by high concrete wall and follow the asphalt road up to the crest of the hill *(alto 550m)* s/o over **crosstracks** [1.0 km]. ▲ *[Detour: Monte Aro visible up right +0.9 km (1.8 km return). A new radio mast mars the ancient castro (now only visible in outline) but the 360° viewpoint remains].*

Continue through line of windmills and take track **right>** [0.3 km] into woodland. Keep s/o (left) at fork and s/o over track [1.9 km] past picnic area and [🏠] (left) into **Pidre** [0.7 km] past Romanesque ***Igrexa S. Xoan*** IX. *[At this point we are 1.1 km from •P **Virxe da O** x6 €50 menú ¶ ℂ 600 065 083 in Quintáns. Refurbished pension midway (+1.5 km) between the main (yellow) and alternative (green) routes opp. the tiny chapel dedicated to Virxe da O].* Continue by road over río Mazaricos *(municipal swim-pool - left)* up into:

4.9 km A Picota *centro* ●*Alb.* **Picota** *Priv.[6÷1]* €15 +2 €35 ℂ 981 852 019 opp. popular ¶ & •*H* **Casa Jurjo** *x20* €40-60 ℂ Jorge 981 852 015 *www.casajurjo.com* (free pickup from Maroñas see photo>). Top of town +**400m** •*Apt.* **Camino Finisterre** *Priv. [10÷1]* €20 +2 €35-45 José ℂ 678 621 047 c/ Cine 3. The waymarked *complentario camino verde* continues

along main road to turn off right> [1.5 km] onto wide track that winds its way along the río Mazaricos back to the road in Mallon [2.3 km] Total 3.8 km.

3.8 km **Mallon** see next page for ●*Alb.* **Ponte Olveira.**

▲ For the main waymarked route turn right> by signboard and <left at **T-junction** [0.8 km] and again <**left** [0.4 km] (road route continues s/o) steeply up new track turning right past **viewpoint** [0.5 km] *(track to summit of Monte Aro)* fine views over the reservoir *Embalse da Fervenza*. The track now starts to descend to sharp turn <**left** [1.1 km] (road route joins at this point) and continue into **Lago** [0.3 km]

3.1 km **Lago** quiet hamlet with delightful ⊣ & ●*Alb.* **Monte Aro** *Priv.[28÷1]* €14 +1 €60 ℭ Tania 881 005 932 / 682 586 157 *www.alberguemontearo.com* opp. welcoming ⚓ *Casa Xalleiro* Juan y Lorena ℭ 981 852 881. *[Note* ❶ *this is the closest ½ way lodging between* **Negreira** *(27.6 km) and* **Cee** *(25.3 km)* ❷ *Free pick-up for Casa Jurjo – see opposite].* The route winds along a series of country lanes through **Portaliñas** [1.0 km] (seating area) and **Abeleiros** [0.4 km]. *[2.9 km by road to A Picota (left)].* Continue onto old asphalt road into **Corzón** [1.4 km] Igrexa de San Cristóbal. ⛺*Camping Corzón [plans for an albergue].* Over to the right are the Montes de la Ruña and the highest peak Monte do Castelo/ Ruña (645m) site of an ancient castle with legends of buried gold!]. Turn <left by cemetery to cross *río Mazariscos* and water mill *Muíño de Mallon* (left). Turn right> in the village of **Mallon** [1.1 km].

3.9 km **Ponte Olveira** *Mallon* on corner of main road is popular albergue. ●*Alb.* **Ponte Olveira** *Priv.[14÷2]* €14 +7 €40+ ℭ 981 852 135 (Alba) m: 603 450 145. Continue s/o over the **río Xallas** *Concello de Dumbria* to *Alb.* **O Refuxio** (currently closed). Continue along main road and shortly after passing the sign (right) for Olveira (*not* OlveirOa) pass •*Hs* **Casa Garrido** B&B from €15 ℭ 674 260 638 *(also own O Peregrino in Olveiroa)* and take the slip road <left into Olveiroa centre:

2.3 km **Olveiroa** *Alb.*❶ **Casa Manola** *Priv.[18÷3]* €15 ℭ 981 741 745 chic new hostal & ⊣ *www.casamanola.com* ❷**Hórreo** *Priv.[58÷7]* €14 ℭ 981 741 673 adj. •*CR* **Casa Loncho** *x12* €30-45 *www.casaloncho.com* all facilities incl. ⚓/⊣, laundry, taxi. ❸ **Olveiroa** *Xunta.* *[40÷5]* €8 ℭ 981 744 001 (Puri) one of the more inspiring Xunta hostels,

reconstructed from traditional houses on either side of quiet village lane. Adj. ❹ ⚓/*bar* **O Peregrino** *Priv.[12÷1]* €12 ℭ 981 741 682. ❺ **Santa Lucía** *Priv. [10÷2]* €12 *x4* €25-35 ℭ 683 190 767 (Fernando). Finally •*P*⁓**As Pías** €40-60 ℭ 981 741 520 *www.aspias.net* handsomely reconstructed traditional stone house with ⚓/⊣ *Bar* and terrace that gets the evening sun.

Ermita S. Lucía [+1.0 km]

Lucía

Cadro

OLVEIROA

N

DP-3404

❺ Lucía

Xunta ❹   ❸ *Peregrino* (Garrido)

❷**Hórreo** ❶**Loncho**

DP-3404

Sunset

❶ℭ **As Pías**

❶⊣❶ **Manola**

† *Iglesia de Santiago*

CAMINO GUIDES.COM

Olveiroa is a quintessential Galician village with traditional stone houses. The village 'square' has a collection of interesting *hórreos* and just beyond is the parochial church **Igrexa Santiago XII** with statue of Saint James above the west door. Taxi service between hostels and places of interest in the area available from Taxi Loncho in Olveiroa © 981 741 673 m: 617 026 005.

Some local detours as follows:

❶ *Santa Lucía* **+1.0** km (2 km return) a short detour off the main road is the tiny hermitage of Santa Lucía adj. the river and fountain of the same name. *[Here an endearing tradition is to heal eye ailments by washing them in the clear spring waters and dry them on a cloth, which is then left out to air – an allusion to drying the tears of remorse at past wrongs in order to heal spiritual blindness and refresh psyche & soul].*

❷ *Dolmen Perxubeira* **+1.9** km. Erected 4000 years ago as a site of sacred ritual and worship. Easily accessed but little visited. *Directions*: From albergue Santa Mariña continue on main road in direction of Muros / Pino do Val *past* the turn-off (right) for Bon Xesus and Forxas/Abaxio to junction (left) Corbeira/Eirón. The dolmen is 200m down a track to the side of the large two-storey house on the corner. It is located in a field (private land – show due care and respect) on the far side of the young plantation. Return the same way. *(Casa Jurjo can arrange a visit).*

❸ *Igrexa de Santiago Ameixenda and Falls of Ézaro (see next stage).*

REFLECTIONS:

_____
_____
_____
_____
_____
_____
_____
_____
_____
_____
_____
_____
_____
_____
_____
_____
_____
_____
_____
_____
_____
_____
_____
_____
_____
_____
_____
_____
_____
_____
_____
_____
_____
_____
_____
_____
_____
_____

3 OLVEIROA – FINISTERRE *centro*

▓▓▓▓	--- ---	21.1	--- ---	68%
▬▬▬	--- ---	8.2	--- ---	26%
▬▬▬	--- ---	<u>1.9</u>	--- ---	6%
Total km		**31.2 km** (19.4 ml)		

Total Ascent 460 m ± *46 mins*
Alto.m ▲ Alto Fabrica 385m *(1,280 ft)*
< 🅰 🅷 > ➲Logoso **3.6** km ➲Hospital **5.5**
➲Cee **18.2** ➲Corcubión **19.8** ➲S. Roque
22.1 ➲Estorde **24.2** ➲Sardiñiero **25.2** km.

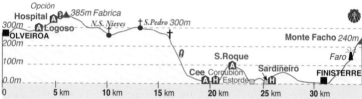

The Practical Path: Another long day if we are headed direct for Finisterre (note the lighthouse *Faro* is a further 3.5 km beyond the town centre). If tiredness overtakes there is plenty of interim lodging and extensive facilities in Cee. The route splits in Hospital for the Muxía option. *[**Note:** if you intend to go direct to Muxía see map on p.88 for this counter-clockwise route].* 70% of the route to Finisterre is on natural pathways including one of the most beautiful and isolated stages on the whole camino with no facilities whatsoever on this spectacular stretch of 12.2 km until Cee.

The Mystical Path: *Faith is the substance of things hoped for; the evidence of things not seen. **Hebrews 11.1**.* What purpose brought us this far? Without faith we are lost indeed. To walk through this life without a spiritual focus is to travel down a cul-de-sac called despair with only our own mortality waiting for us at the end. To walk the inner camino with a pure motive and openness of mind is to journey to the source of our own immortality. Will we take time today to reflect on the purpose of our life and the means of fulfilling it? *The final lesson for each soul is the total surrender to the Will of God manifested in our own hearts.*

Personal Notes: "... too exhausted to undo the straps on my backpack I collapsed at the side of the road. The last thing I remembered was the rain falling on my face. When I came round the spasm in my lower back had gone. I was lying at the foot of a medieval cross with a figure of Christ crucified looking down at me. It is strange; I had not noticed it before..."

0.0 km Leaving Olveiroa *centro* past •*As Pias* turn <left over stream *río Santa Lucía* and follow track onto open moorland with extensive views up

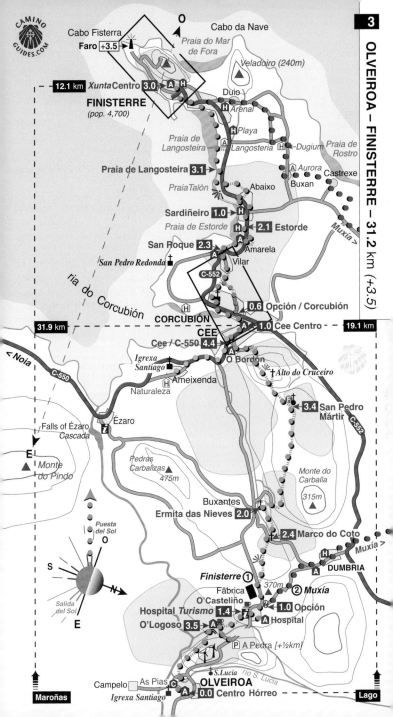

the río Xallas valley (left) which widens here to form a small reservoir *Embalse de Ponte Olveira y Castrelo*. Continue along track towards wind-farm through young forest plantation and follow the contour line west over *rio do Hospital* [**Detour** *left to 'Balance Stone'* **Pedra Cabalada** *+600m]*. Turn up right into:

3.5 km Logoso hamlet with welcoming ⛲/●*Alb*. **Logoso** *Priv.[32÷4]* €15 *+10* €35-40 Ⓒ 981 727 602 (Domingo). *[The family also run the nearby apartments at A Pedra* Ⓒ 652 864 623 *x7* apt./rooms from €35-55 *on main road +0.6 km]*. Veer <left up track to rejoin the main road in Hospital.

1.4 km Hospital ❶*Turismo Centro de Información ao Peregrino de Hospital* (Dumbría) Ⓒ 981 744 001. *[The village supported a pilgrim hospital in the medieval period and was subsequently raised to the ground by Napoleon's troops during the peninsular war]*. In 2015 the village finally renovated a replacement hostel (300m *off* route) *down* main road in lower end of Hospital village. ●*Alb*. **Hospital** *Priv.[20÷3]* €14 *+1* €20 Managed by Javier (son of Marina) Ⓒ 981 747 387 who welcomes pilgrims and provides the reception for the hostel at ⛲ *O Casteliño* directly on the waymarked route [**0.4** km] *up* the main road where Marina takes bookings and provides a 'last chance saloon' before venturing onto the open moorland beyond. The popular café also serves the nearby factory *Fábrica*. The camino now follows a bend in the old road to our high point at 370m **Alto [0.6** km]:

1.0 km Cruce *Opción* here the route splits – West (left) for Finisterre or s/o North for Muxía. A marker on the central reservation (see photo>) indicates Fisterra 28 km / Muxía 27 km (Finisterre *lighthouse* / Muxía *sanctuary* respectively, *not* the town centres). If you plan to visit both (each has its unique flavour and pilgrimage tradition) there are advantages in proceeding clockwise to Finisterre and then continuing to Muxía. This way around you ① walk downhill

over the moors with the first dramatic views of the sea and Cabo Finisterre. ② benefit from an equally beautiful entry into Muxía along the coast from Finisterre and ③ Muxía provides a quieter space *off* the main camino for rest and reflection before returning home (by bus or taxi). If you are returning on foot as part of the camino 'circuit' note waymarking is in *both* directions so extra vigilance is required. Whichever route you take there are challenges... and rewards.

If you decide to walk anti-clockwise direct to Muxía go to map on page 88.

For Finisterre turn <left by the unsightly carbide factory whose chimneys spew smoke making it visible for miles around. Trucks laden with iron ore

thunder up and down the road between here and the industrial port in Cee. Opp. the factory car-park we turn off **right>** [**0.6** km] onto the ancient Royal Way *Camino Real* and leave the incongruous factory behind us to pass over these isolated moors for a mystical 12.3 km.

Nearby are prehistoric stone carvings *Pedra Longa* engraved 4,000 years ago and the megalithic monuments *mamoas* and dolmens dotted around this sacred landscape. All bear witness to the antiquity of this route that our pagan forebears walked centuries before the Christian era dawned. This is also one of the areas associated with the mythical Vakner, '... *a terrifying creature, man-like, of a malignant nature, that lives like a troglodyte in the deepest and densest parts of the forest.*' It is suggested this mythic creature was used by the early Church to discourage the practise of pagan rites here. The mythic figure was probably based on the sighting of wild boar or bear that may have roamed these high moors. To heighten the sense of foreboding we can add the following myth of the assembly of departed souls *Estadéa* that wander about here visiting those who are to join them – referred to as the Holy Company *Santa Compaña* by H.V. Morton in *A Stranger in Spain*:

> *When you are travelling at night in Galicia, you may in certain marshy places see flickering lights which dart here and there over the mournful landscape. You must now be very careful. It may be that you will find an invisible presence trying to place a lighted candle in your hand, and should you open your hand and accept it, you are lost... So it can happen that you may simply disappear from life and spend an eternity trying to get rid of your candle, haunting the moorlands and the waste places where the ghostly lights flicker, until at last you can lure some human being into the Holy Company of Souls and escape yourself!'*

This is the high point of today's stage and providing you escape the *Vakner* and the *Santa Compaña* you will have your first view of the sea (providing you are also spared the rain or hill fog that *does* frequent this high moor). The path now slopes gently downhill through scrub-land, mostly gorse and heather with pockets of young forestry to **road** [**1.8** km]:

2.4 km **Marco do Couto** here we cross over road with 18thC wayside *cruceiro* and adj. medieval marker-stone with the initials *RC* (likely reference to the Royal Way to Finisterre *Real Camino*). The waymarked route now follows the contour line before dropping down <left to:

2.0 km **Ermita Nosa Señora das Nieves** 18thC *Hermitage of Our Lady of the Snows* and site of an annual local pilgrimage *romería* each September to this remote chapel and Holy Spring by the ancient stone cross in the field immediately below. The waters are said to have healing properties, particularly effective for nursing mothers. From here we cross over the 'river of snows' *Riego do Nievas* and make our way uphill to traverse the hillside opposite and join a track (right) **[2.6 km]** where we continue by the edge of mature woodland past abandoned farm buildings to **hermitage [0.8** km]:

`3.4 km` **Ermita San Pedro Martír** [🏠] *Fuente San Pedro Martír* hermitage with shelter, water font and picnic area. Not to be outdone by Our Lady of the Snows – Saint Peter the Martyr cures bodily aches and rheumatism with the simple expedient of placing the diseased part of the body in the waters of the holy spring. The route continues along the ridge of the hill to **Cruceiro do Armada [2.2** km] the original stone cross has gone but a substitute marks the spot (100m *off* route).

From here we get the first views over the *rias* of Cee and Corcubion with Monte Facho and Cabo Finisterre on the distant horizon (see photo) now partly obscured by the woodland plantation. Continue very steeply [!] downhill on a rocky track that winds its way through the pine-woods to an asphalt road **[1.7** km] turn <left down to T-junction **[0.2** km] where

(50m left *off* route) on the outskirts of **Os Camiños Chans (Cee)** is *Alb.*❶ **O Bordón** *Priv.[24÷1]* €15 © 981 197 562 (Pedro) m: 655 903 932. To continue towards Cee turn right> at T-junction to pass wayside cross to the main road at **Os Camiños Chans [0.3** km].

`4.4 km` C-550 / **Os Camiños Chans / Cee** *Options* ☕ *Casa Talieiro* first café in 13.2 km so popular with pilgrims! Camiños Chans is the industrial port of Cee with several **Options:** (see town map).
Ⓐ Follow waymarks through **Cee** via shops & hotels to **Corcubión [1.9** km].
Ⓑ Follow the beach around the coast direct to **Corcubión [0.6** km].
● *Detour:* to *Ameixenda* **[2.8** km] & *Falls of Ézaro* **[11** km] see next page.

To continue on the waymarked route turn right> along busy *Ruta Atlántica* C-550 past •**Mar no Camiño** €70+ © 617 889 641 with sea views at Nº5. Keep s/o and veer <left immediately past cemetery past *Pietà* (left) and 🍴*Angueira* (right). Turn right here for main route or s/o for beach route.

`1.0 km` **Cee** *Options* If you don't intend to stay or visit Cee town a good option is to take the coast route Ⓑ ● ● ● direct to Corcubion. **Directions:** Keep s/o down the steps in front *Alb.*❷ **Moreira** *Priv.[14÷2]* €15 +4 €35 ©981 746 282 (José Manuel) on c/ Rosalia de Castro, 75 with fine views over the bay is on our left at this point. Continue over the main Paseo Marítimo to the town beach *Praia da Concha*. Cee town centre with modern shopping mall and hospital are over to our right at this point. Continue up into Corcubión.

Ⓐ *To visit Cee* or if you intend staying the night turn right> into r/Magdalena *(new prominent signposting)* pass ⑂/•*H*¨**Larry** *x21* €32-45 Ⓒ 981 746 441 r/Madgdelena,8 (left) to •*Pazo do Cotón y Cruceiro da Fonte Penín (drinking font at rear)* and *Alb.*Ⓑ **A Casa da Fonte** *Priv.[40÷1]* €14 Ⓒ 981 746 663 r/Arriba, 36. Continue s/o towards town centre past *Alb.* Ⓒ

Tequerón *Priv.[14÷2]* €15 Pilar Ⓒ 666 119 594. Turn <left down steps into the tiny Plaza Olvido emerging in Praza da Constitución 🕭*Bar Atrio* with outside seating and •*Iglesia de Nuestra Señora da Xunqueira* (see photo above) restored XV[th]C parish church *[and monument to the town's famous architect Domingo de Andrade who also designed the clock tower in Santiago cathedral]*.

Continue over roundabout at Plaza Mercado into Rua 'A' past •*H* **La Marina** *x32* €40-60 Ⓒ 981 746 511 *www.hotellamarina.com* turn <left into Av. Fernando Blanco and <left into Av. Finisterre *[Note: Alb. Estrelas & Casa Crego closed]* pass •*H*¨¨**Oca Insua** *x50* €45-50 Ⓒ 981 747 575 *www.hotelinsua. com* and where we join the coast •*P*¨**Beiramar** *x8* €40-50 Ⓒ 981 745 040 Av. Finisterre, 220 (also own *Alb.***Camiño Fisterra** see Corcubión).

Cee: bustling commercial town serving the local fishing and industrial port with a resident population of 7,500. Like so many of the towns and villages in this part of Galicia it was largely destroyed by the French troops of Napoleon in the early 1800's but reminders of its historic past remain in the buildings and monuments and its narrow winding streets such as the typical Rúa Rosalía de Castro with the XVIII[th]c facades of the Casa Mosteirín and adjoining Casa Mayá. Most of the restaurants and bars can be found around the wide Paseo Maritimo with modern shopping centre and main bus station with regular services to and from Finisterre and Santiago.

● *Detour:* **3.2** km by road – share a taxi? ● *Igrexa de Santiago da Ameixenda* The church has a statue of *Santiago Matamoros* and small reliquary reputedly containing a piece of St. James fingernail obtained during the removal of his body from Dugium to Libredon and associated with yet more miracles in this deeply religious part of Galicia. Contact Concello in Cee Ⓒ 981 745 100 for opening hours. ***Directions*** from **Os Camiños Chans** 🕭 *Casa Talieiro* turn left along the main road over the bridge in Pontella [1.0 km] and turn off <left [1.5 km] up towards the village of Ameixenda. The church of Santiago is at the far end [0.7 km] opp. •*H* **De Naturaleza** *x20* €60+ Ⓒ 645 823 993 on the outskirts. Return the same way *or* continue *a further* 8.2 km along the main road to ● *Falls of Ézaro* the only river (*río Xallas*) in Europe that flows directly into the sea as a waterfall. Situated in a dramatic location at the foot of Monte Pindo (see under myths). ❶ *Turismo* c/Río do Barco Ⓒ 662 346 927. •*H* **Mar do Ézaro** *x8* €48+ Ⓒ 981 194 416 c/Río Xallas 103, Ézaro.

`0.6 km` **Corcubión** *more options! See plan:*
🅐 continue on main route which follows the original 'medieval' route through the old town.
🅑 Follow path parallel to the coast road.
🅒 take the scenic upper path above the town.
🅓 detour (off route) to the beach and hotels in *Praia de Quenxe.* All routes join, after a steep climb in **San Roque** c.2½ km.

Corcubión: is an attractive seaside town designated site of 'National Cultural Interest' with a population of 1,700 serving a busy summer tourist trade.

🅐 ● ● ● ● The newly waymarked main route now follows the original 'medieval' way through the old town. Take the road up steeply by the Corcubión sign to pass *Alb.* ❺ **Camiño Fisterra** *Priv.[14÷1]* €10 ☎ 981 745 040 c/ Cruceiro de Valdomar, 11 (**check if open**). Continue up and veer <left past viewpoint and into Rúa Rafael Juan where @N°44 ▲ is the welcoming •*CR* **Casa da Balea** *x6* €40-50 ☎ 652 424 200 *www.casadabalea. com.* Continue down into **Praza de Castelao** passing Capilla del Pilar (right) and ¶*Pulperia* & •*P* **Mar Viva** *x6* €55+ ☎ 981 745 325 *www.pensionmarviva. com* Pl. José Carrera, 4.

🅑 ● ● ● ● Continue by coast path parallel to the main road C-445 passing •*H* `El Hórreo` (possibly still closed) into **Praza de Castelao**.

Both routes join in **Praza de Castelao** with several cafes and continue up past Taxi rank ☎ 981 745 023 into c/Castelao and up into Praza San Marcos with its fine XII[th]c romanesque parish church •**Igrexa San Marcos [0.9** km] *[Corcubión had extensive sea trade with Italy and Venice, hence the celebration of San Marcos].* In the church square Plaza Párroco Francisco Sánchez,3 •*CR* **Casa de Bernarda** *x3* €35-70 ☎ 981 747 157.

🅒 ● ● ● ● For the upper route along woodland paths above the town take the steps up right> directly *opposite* ▲ •**Casa da Balea** past the recently restored •**Capela de San Antonio** *XVII (often open).* Continue along the lane by house N° 14 (*not* up to Cuartel Gardia Civil). Follow the lane s/o left keeping the contour until it joins the main route by narrow lane (left) **Rúa Fontiñas**.

🅓 ● ● ● ● Detour (off route) to the beach and hotels in *Praia de Quenxe.* From **Praza de Castelao** keep on around the headland into Porto de Corcubión *Turismo* (summer) 🛈 *O Carrumeiro* and continue along seaside path leading to access to the lovely sandy cove *Praia de Quenxe* ½ km off route with popular ¶/•*H* **As Hortensias** *x16* €30-40 ☎ 981 747 584 with beach access and •*H* **Praia de Quenxe** *x8* €35+ ☎ 676 745 134. You can also access the port area and *Praia de Quenxe* by taking the road immediately to the rear of **Igrexa San Marcos Praza San Marcos** (see town plan)

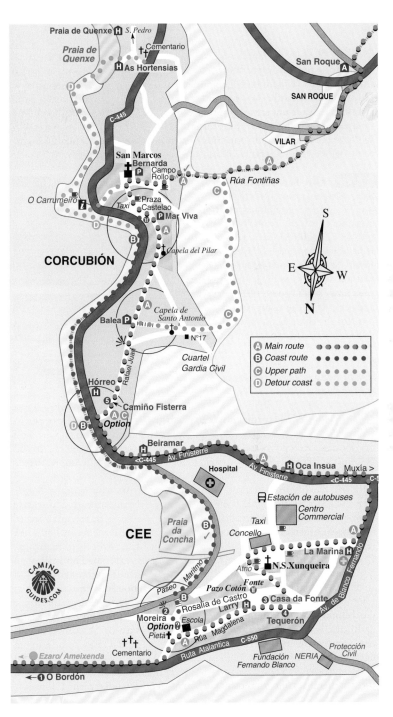

Ⓐ ● ● ● ● From •**Igrexa San Marcos** [**0.9** km] continue up the steps right> into Rua As Mercedes with well preserved houses bearing armorial shields into the wide square Campo do Rollo [🛈] *Fuente Rollo* 🪧 *Bujeiro*. Cross the square and head up the steep narrow lane to join wide track in the pine forest ahead (the alternative scenic route joins from the right). Continue up steeply to join an asphalt road turning right> into the hamlet of **Vilar** [**0.8** km] and proceed up to the top and over the main road for the final [**0.6** km] to the windswept high point of this stage:

2.3 km **Alto San Roque** *Vilar* ●*Alb.* **San Roque** *Asoc.[14÷2]* €-donation ℂ 679 460 942 communal meal may be available (no local shops, buy provisions in Cee/Corcubion). Managed by AGAC *Associación Galician Amigos del Camino*. Just beyond the albergue we pick up our first real view of the cape of Finisterre.The way now heads downhill playing hide-and-seek with the main road cutting off some of the sharp bends around the steep coastal inlets. The woodland path rejoins the main road at **Amarela** passing ●*Alb.* **San Pedro** *Priv.[4÷1]*€15 +2 €40+ ℂ 670 395 045. and continues down to the beach at:

2.1 km **Playa de Estorde** fine sandy bay with ¶/•*H*¨**Playa de Estorde** *x15* €40-60 ℂ 981 745 585 *www.restauranteplayadeestorde.com* with popular 🪧/¶ overlooking the beach. Opposite ▲*Camping* **Ruta Finisterre** ℂ 981 746 302 (summer) Continue along main road or cross over for short detour into:

1.0 km **Sardiñeiro** The route crosses back over the main road by ¶/•*H*¨ **Playa de Sardiñeiro** *x16* €40-60 ℂ 981 743 741. Access beach and seaside park to rear with 🪧 *A Cabaña* and *Mesón Cabanel* (entrance main road). Continue on main road *[300m off route to access* •*H* **Merendero** *x20* €20-35 *pilgrim price €12 pp* ℂ *981 743 535]*. Continue back over main road (sign Praia do Rostro) up along narrow concrete road *rúa de Fisterra* through **Sardiñero de Abaixo** onto a woodland path that winds up through pine and eucalyptus plantation for a delightful stretch away from the main road to rejoin at **Punto de Vista** [**2.0** km] wonderful viewpoint of Cabo Finisterre and Monte Pindo. Cross the main road [!] ***dangerous bend*** onto narrow path above the beach of **Talón** (steep steps down to this lovely isolated beach) and rejoin main road veering down <left on the lane-way by stone column *Corredoira de Don Camilo* and •*H*¨¨**Alen do Mar** *x11* €60-105 ℂ 981 740 745 *www.hotelalendomar.com* modern luxury hotel set back from the beach in the woodland at Calcoba overlooking the delightful sandy beach [**1.1** km] at:

3.1 km **Praia Langosteira** with its 2 kilometres of pure white sand.

> *Along a beach of dazzling white sand we advanced towards the cape, the bourne of our journey... it was upon this beach that, according to the tradition of all ancient Christendom, Saint James, the patron saint of Spain, preached the gospel to the heathen Spaniards. 'What is the name of this village?' said I to a woman as we passed by five or six ruinous houses at the bend of the bay, ere we entered upon the peninsular of Finisterre, 'This is no village, said the Gallegan, this is a city, this is Duyo.' So much for the glory of the world. These huts were all that the roaring sea and the tooth of time had left of Duyo, the great city! Onward now to Finisterre.* The Bible in Spain *George Borrow.*

Take off your boots, feel the sand under your feet, swim, laugh, cry – congratulations, you have arrived at the end of the way and the world – well, almost! You are now only 2.5 km from the centre of Finisterre (6 km from the lighthouse – both clearly visible ahead). Walk the beach or take the waymarked route along the paved

walkway through the pine trees (photo below) directly ahead parallel to the main road with lodging in **Anchoa** as follows:

●*Alb.***Langosteira** *Priv.[16÷1]* €10 © 618 065 387 (Basic – *still closed?*) Just past it (and just open) overlooking the beach is ultra-modern •*H*```Bela *x16* €70+ © 981 110 311 *www. belafisterra.com* further along the main road •*H*```**Playa Langosteira** *x28* €35-55 © 981 706 830 Lugar de Escaselas, **Anchoa** also •*H*`**Arenal** €35+ © 981 740 208 Rúa Cabello. Both routes

join at the far end of the beach at **San Roque** at ¶ *Tira do Cordell* where you can watch the fishermen and women bringing their produce straight from the sea to the kitchen – expensive but exquisite (fish and mariscos doesn't come fresher than this). Adj. ¶/•*P* **Doña Lubina** *x9* €30-50 © 981 740 311 *www.donalubina.com* concrete path brings us up past •*H* **Mar de Fisterra** *x16* €70+ © 981 740 204 *www.hotelmardefisterra.com* on Rua S.Roque with terrace overlooking the sea. Pass viewpoint by wayside cross at **Baximar** from where we can look back over the sweeping curve of the Praia de Langosteira and the backdrop of mountains that brought us here (see photo p.44). Follow the main road past •*H* **Langosteira** *x11* €35-45 © 981 740 543 *www. hotellangosteira.com* Av. Coruña, 61 overlooking the sea and adj. 🍺 *bar World Family*. Where the main road veers right we continue s/o into the old town along pedestrian street **Av. Coruña** with *Coviran* supermarket (left) @**N°33** *Alb.* **❶** Oceanus *Priv.[38÷2]* €15 +2 €40 Ⓒ 981 740 068 / 609 821 302 _www.oceanusfinisterre.es_ @**N°13** **❷** Cabo Vila *Priv.[32÷2]* €15 +9 €30-€40 Ⓒ 981 740 454 m: 607 735 474 Alexia, Nita & Alejandra. Up steps (right) opp. *Correos*: •*P* López *x8* €15+pp Ⓒ 981 740 449. Continue past council offices *Concello (issue Fisteranna)* down **Calle Santa Catalina** @**N°44** •*Hs''* **Mariquito** *x17* €30-45 Ⓒ 981 740 044 with 🍴/*bar* and emerge at the central square with the municipal albergue on the corner opposite.

3.0 km Finisterre *Centro Alb.* **❸**

Xunta [26÷2] €8 Ⓒ 981 740 781 corner of c/ Real 2. Maintained by the local council and managed by Begoña and volunteers. Open 13:00 (15:00 winter) just time to shed backpacks to explore the headland & lighthouse a further 3.5 km up Monte Facho. Central location close to all amenities and bus-stop for return journey to Santiago; unless you're planning to walk back via Mux**í**a *(pron: MushEEah)*. *Concello* certificate of completion **Fisterrana** available to pilgrims who have walked from Santiago (a stamped *credencial* is essential). **RETURN SANTIAGO:** Several daily buses ± €10 travel time ± 3 hours depending on route. •***Monbus*** Ⓒ 982 292 900 _www.monbus.es/en_ via Cee / Muros •***Arriva*** Ⓒ 981 311 213 _www.arriva.gal_ via Muxia + •***Ferrin*** Ⓒ 981 873 643 _www.grupoferrin.com_ via Negreira. •***Taxi Central***: 24 hours Ⓒ 666 862 373 _www.taxifisterra.es_ – Santiago ±1¼ hours ± €100.

Other Albergues: **❹** Por Fin *Priv.[11÷3]* €15 +1 €32 Ⓒ 636 764 726 Hungarian hostel Aranka Rósa c/Federico Ávila,19. **❺** Mar de Rostro *Priv. [23÷2]* €14 Pilar y Nazareth Ⓒ 637 107 765 c/Alcade Fernandez,45. **❻** Buen Camino *Priv.[50÷7]* €15+ +sauna Ⓒ 981 740 771 Sonia c/ Atalaya, 11. **❼** Sol e Lúa *Priv.[15÷3]* €15 +3 €25+ quiet space + large garden Ⓒ 617 568 648 Miguel c/ Atalaya, 7. **❽** Mar de Fora *Priv.[34÷5]* €12+/ +2 €35+ sun terrace Ⓒ 648 263 639 r/Potiña, 14. **❾** Espiral *Priv.[12÷2]* €14 +2 €30+ Ⓒ 607 684 248 (Fátima / Yaiza) Fonte Vella, 19 adj. **❿** O Encontro *Priv. [14÷2]* €12+ +4 €40+ Ⓒ 696 503 363 Soraya e Hilda c/Fonte Vella, 22. **⓫** A Pedra Santa *Priv.[22÷3]* €14 Trad. town house Ⓒ 615 170 488 Travesía de Arriba, 6. **⓬** Arasolis *Priv.[16÷2]* €14 +3 €20+ Ⓒ 638 326 869 c/Ara Solis, 3. **⓭** Finistellae *Priv.[20÷2]* €12+6 €30-35 Ⓒ 637 821 296 c/ Manuel Lago Pais, 7. **⓮** Paz *Priv.[14÷2]* €15 +3 €35+ Ⓒ 981 740 332 m: 628 903 693 c/ Victor Cardalda, 11.**⓯** Fin da Terra e Camiño *Priv.[12÷3]* €15 +7 €25-30 Ⓒ 675 361 890 c/Alfredo Saralegui, 15.

Other hotels: Central on c/Federico Ávila @N°8 •*H'* **Vida Finisterre** *x30* €40-50 Ⓒ 981 740 000 / 881 098 207 & @N°7 •*P* **Cabo** *x12* €20-30 Ⓒ 981 740 671. By roundabout on r/Alcalde Fernández @N°55 •*Hs''* **Rivas** *x15* €25-45 Ⓒ 981 740 027 _www.hostalrivas.com_ @N°43 •*H'* **Áncora** *x30* €35+

© 981 740 791 *www.hotelancorafinisterre.com* Near Xunta alb. •*P* **Casiña de Dina** *x1* €75 *©* 667 916 034 entire house top floor bedroom with views over harbour. 24 Rúa Real. By harbour •*H* **Banco Azul** €60+ *©* 981 712 391 *hoteldobancoazul.com* rúa Pescadores 1. ¶/•*P*˙**Casa Velay** Rúa de Cerca *©* 981 740 127. •*P*˙ **Fin da Terra** c/Atalaia *©* 981 712 030. •*P* **Mirador Fin da Terra** *x9* €38+ *©* 648 918 929 c/Montarón. •*H*¨**Prado da Vina** *x12* €35-55 *©* 981 740 326 Camino Barcia. •*H*¨**Rústico Ínsua Finisterrae** €35-75 *©* 981 712 211 camino Insua, 128 near back beach and •*H*¨*Spa* **Mar de Ardora** *x6* €90+ 667 641 304 c/ Potiña, 15. ¶/•*H*¨**O Semaforo** *x6* €99 *©* 981 110 210 *www.hotelsemaforodefisterra.com* adj. lighthouse.

Restaurants: are plentiful with fresh fish and shellfish *mariscos* a speciality. The ubiquitous TV and harsh neon lighting doesn't help the ambience, ¶ *Tira do Cordel* at Baixamar comes closest to the authentic gastronomic experience but there is plenty of competition. Amongst the best value is ¶ *Mesón Arco da Vella* on Paseo da Ribeira with home cooking from Carmen and a first floor terrace overlooking the harbour (arrive early if you want a table).

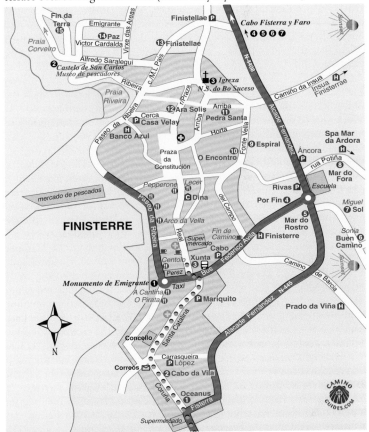

Finisterre a busy fishing port with a resident population of 4,700 that expands during the summer months as tourists and pilgrims converge on the town with its range of shops, bars, restaurants and hotels. While the town is sheltered from the worst of the westerly gales it has nevertheless been ravaged by wind, rain and pirates down through the centuries, consequently there is little of historic or artistic significance remaining. However the town's somewhat 'untidy' layout and modernity overlies a rich historical past.

Note: If you have walked from Olveiroa you will likely want to shower and rest before tackling (perhaps the next day) the 9.9 km round-trip of Cabo Finisterre including the famous lighthouse (now a popular tourist attraction) but the headland also invites exploration of the less well known historic and mythical sites. Each specific spot has a number that corresponds to its location on the map so you can readily identify each one. Your decision might rest on practical realities such as the state of the weather. If you are blessed with a clear sky it may be worth the effort to join the crowds at the lighthouse or climb Monte Facho or the less strenuous option to walk over to the back-beach, the Outer Sea *Mar de Fora* to watch the sun sink below the Western horizon... or take a tour of the town, have a drink with friends, or both? Descriptions of these various options are detailed on the following pages.

■ **Town Centre and Charles Fort 1.0 km *(round trip)*.** Allow a couple of hours for a leisurely stroll around the lively harbour area. From the albergue pass the evocative Monument to the Emigrant ❶ *Monumento de Emigrante* (see photo above) and continue down to the fish market *Mercado de Pescado* resembling the lines of Finisterre's modern fishing fleet. You can visit the fish market and information display on the first floor (small entrance fee). Continue along the seafront to the austere fortified tower of Harbour House overlooking the town beach *Praia de Ribeira* with St. Charles Castle ❷ *Castelo de San Carlos XVIII* located above the entrance to the sandy bay. This strategic castle was recently converted to a fishing museum *museo de pescadores* with artefacts and historical information recognising the importance of the fishing industry to this part of Galicia. The canon a stark reminder of its military past. Not many continue to the viewpoint located behind the fort that overlooks the tiny cove *Praia Corbeiro* with sandy beach.

It is delightfully easy to get lost in the narrow back lanes but the sea is never far away so you might return via the baroque chapel of the Good Event ❸ *Capela do Bo Suceso XVII* located at the original heart of the town in *Praza Ara-Solis*. Here we also find Quadrant House *XIII* an former pilgrim hospital. Continue back along c/Ara-Solis to *Plaza da Constitución* and return to the municipal albergue via the Royal Way *Calle Real*.

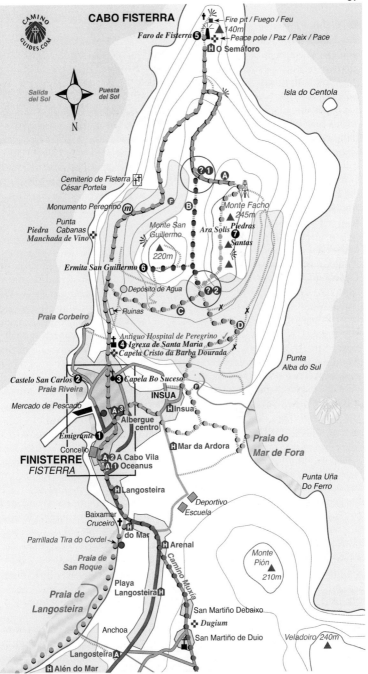

CABO FISTERRA

Fire pit / Fuego / Feu
140m
Peace pole / Paz / Paix / Pace

Faro de Fisterra 5
O Semáforo

Isla do Centola

Salida
del Sol

Puesta
del Sol

N

? 1 A

Cemiterio de Fisterra
César Portela

Monumento Peregrino (m)

F

B

Monte Facho
245m

Punta
Piedra Cabanas
Manchada de Vino

Monte San
Guillermo

Ara Solis

Piedras
7 Santas

220m

Ermita San Guillermo 6

Depósito de Agua

? 2

Praia Corbeiro

Ruinas

C

D

Antiguo Hospital de Peregrino
4 *Igrexa de Santa Maria*
Capela Cristo da Barba Dourada

Punta
Alba do Sul

Castelo San Carlos 2
Praia Riveira

3 *Capela Bo Suceso*

E

Mercado de Pescado

A 3

INSUA

Insua

Emigrante 1

Albergue
centro

Concello

FINISTERRE
FISTERRA

A 2 A Cabo Vila
A 1 Oceanus

Mar da Ardora

*Praia do
Mar de Fora*

Langosteira

Punta Uña
Do Ferro

Deportivo
Escuela

Baixamar
Cruceiro
do Mar

Parrillada Tira do Cordel

Arenal

*Praia de
San Roque*

Monte
Pión
210m

Playa
Langosteira

*Praia de
Langosteira*

San Martiño Debaixo
Dugium

Anchoa

San Martiño de Duio

Veladoiro 240m

Langosteira A
Alén do Mar

■ **Cabo Finisterre – 3.5** km *(9.9 km round trip via Monte Facho)*: You can of course take any number of alternative routes but the one described here covers the main sites of historic, religious and mythological interest in the shortest distance, commencing with a hike up the asphalt road to the lighthouse and returning via peaceful woodland paths. Allow half a day for the recommended round trip of steep

hilly ground. If you intend to make a thanksgiving or purification ritual then consider staying an extra day as there is much to see and do. Remember it is 3.5 km just to the lighthouse (7.0 km there and back). Note the numbered sites ❹ to ❼ refer to the detailed notes on mythology and are linked to the map of Cabo Finisterre to aid identification.

Leave the albergue up the narrow c/Real and through the main square Plaza Constitución veering right> into the Plaza Ara Solis and <left at the ❸ *Capela do Bo Suceso XVII* [0.4 km] up to join the main road leading to the church of Our Lady of the Sands ❹ *Igrexa de Santa María das Areas XII* [0.5 km] a religious and historical gem. To the rear is the cemetery and the arched remains of the last pilgrim refuge in medieval Christendom. Perhaps you will rest awhile on the stone seating that surrounds the church and take time to pay tribute to the pilgrims who set out to make it to the end of the world – many didn't as pilgrim cemeteries all the way from France attest. Here monks welcomed and cared for the pilgrims from the 11th century – a place, perhaps, to give thanks for your own safe arrival. Like so many churches today it is often locked but worth the effort to check opening times. Inside is a fine statue of **Santiago Peregrino** in the nave (see p.10) and the chapel of Christ of the Golden Beard **Cristo da Barba Dourada** *(see Myths and Legends p.63)*.

Continue uphill past turn-off right> [0.6 km] *[short-cut to the top of Monte Facho]* and s/o up the asphalt road past modern statue of a medieval pilgrim (top photo) ● *Monumento Peregrinos* [0.4 km] and **Fonte Cabanas** [0.1 km] whose clear spring waters gush out of the side of Monte Facho and into the sea at **Punta da Cabanas** the rocky cove below and site of another legend linking Christ with Finisterre *Piedra Manchada de Vino p.63)*. Cemetery *cimiterio (below left)*. It's now a climb to the turn-off (right) [0.9 km] to Monte Facho but keep s/o past the souvenir shops and the marine observatory (now converted to hotel & restaurant **O Semaforo**) adj. the lighthouse [0.5 km].

3.5 km Lighthouse *Faro* ❺ the famed lighthouse at the 'end of the world' has likewise been refurbished and is now a museum and exhibition space with audio-visual display on the history of Finisterre. With the advent of satellite navigation systems the lighthouse is largely redundant although it remains a tracking station for shipping. Outside are various monuments to the 'discovery' of the Americas by European explorers. The most recent and uplifting addition (imm. above the lighthouse) is a *Peace Pole p.64)* planted by the international World Peace Project. Its simple message reads, 'May Peace Prevail On Earth' *Que La Paz Prevalezca En La Tierra* and points heavenward encouraging us to 'think peace to create peace'.

Just below and to the rear of the lighthouse are several pilgrim monuments including the poignant brass boot rooted in the rock face and surrounded by the Atlantic swell that crashes around the headland 126 metres (413 feet) below. The pungent smell, blackened rocks and adjoining fire pit are evidence of 'burnt offerings' left by modern-day pilgrims. A common ritual is to burn an item of old clothing or some written statement that includes attachments or habits no longer wanted or needed and to see the ashes of our past actions blown away so that, like the Phoenix, we can arise anew and fly to ever greater heights (a token piece should suffice; not the whole garment! see fire-pit p.64).

When you are complete with your visit to the Faro make your way back to the souvenir stalls to **Option ✖** and take the path by car-park to join the upper road that climbs steeply to earth track straight ahead and **Option Ⓨ** [**1.2** km]. **Ⓐ** continue up the asphalt road to radio mast and **Monte Facho [0.4** km] and take the wide track along the crest of the hill to the **high point** [**0.4** km] 50m on the left (**Total 2.0** km from Faro). **❼** *Piedras Santas* Here at 240 metres (787 feet) above sea level is an uninterrupted view west over the Atlantic with the horizon at this height around 56 kilometres (35 miles). There are 3 rocky outcrops spread out along the wide forestry track that collectively make up the Sacred Stones *Piedras Santas* and the **Altar to the Sun** *Ara Solis*. Take care when climbing as there are narrow crevices and respect the silence for self and others. The small island just offshore to the south/west is named after the Spider Crab *Centola* also linked to a pagan myth. Return the way you came *or* continue along the wide track and descend via the fire-break to **Option ❷**.

Ⓑ Turn right> onto *path* [**0.7** km] that keeps a level contour line through the gorse that covers much of this modest rise known as **❻** *Monte San Guillermo p.65)* [**0.3** km] (**Total 2.2** km from Faro). the 5th century **Saint William's Hermitage** *Ermita de San Guillerme* 221m (725 feet). This wonderful hermitage site is little visited excepting periodical archaeological investigation but this is unobtrusive and leaves the area largely intact. Take care not to disturb the ancient stonewalls and respect this ancient sacred site. The hermitage is a bare ruin built into the leeward side of the giant boulder sheltering it from the Westerly winds that roar across this headland, protecting it too from the pagan rites associated with Monte Facho. The hermitage faces due East to catch the first rays of the rising sun over the Celtic **'Mount Olympus'** *Monte Pindo* (see photo>).

Several sources state that St. James himself preached from this spot in his efforts to counter the pagan rites associated with the **Ara Solis** *(see Myths p.66)* and the subsequent fertility rites practised here. To access Monte Facho and the **Sacred Stones** return to the main track [**0.3** km] turn right> and continue to a fire break through the pine woods up on your <left [**0.3** km] make your way up rough track for [**0.4** km] to the Piedras Santas (see map).

Alternative return routes from Monte Facho to the town centre:

Ⓐ 4.4 km – The longest route but consider if visibility is poor as it follows the asphalt road back from the wireless station at the southern end of Monte Facho and returns via the lighthouse road but is exposed to wind and rain.

Ⓒ 2.9 km – an alternative is to take a wide woodland track to rejoin the asphalt road above the church of Santa Maria. *[Note: this route is not well waymarked]*. Continue beyond the Piedras Santas and take the rough fire-break back down to the dirt track below and turn <left and imm. right> at the fork [0.4 km] **Option ❷** where the wide forest track runs gently down to pass the town's water supply and continues back down to rejoin the main road [1.1 km] past the church of Santa Maria back to the town centre [1.4 km].

Ⓓ 3.1 km – *[1.7 **Praia do Mar de Fora** + 1.4 km **back to Finisterre**] (via the back beach or 'outer sea' – Praia do Mar de Fora): [Note: this route is not well waymarked]*. Make your way back down the fire-break to the dirt track and turn <left and **s/o** at the fork [0.4 km] **Option ❷** *(ignoring the right-hand track described at 'c' above)* continue to *second* wide sweep left [0.3 km] [**!**] (Do **not** continue s/o down here as there are many steep fishermen's tracks below) At this point you leave the main track and take the narrow stone-lined path that drops steeply down through woodland. This was an original access way to Monte Facho and it certainly has an ancient feel about it. Continue down to the top end of the straggling village of **A Insua** [0.5 km] to Europe's quirkiest shop/bar on the corner (right). *(At this point you can continue s/o back to the centre of Finisterre)* or turn <left at small concrete parking area onto paved footpath (passing the ancient *Fonte Cardal* left – 50m *off* route) and turn <left [200m] onto board-walk to viewpoint above the beach [300m]. Make your way down to the delightful windswept sand and the ocean.

Note: It is dangerous to swim in the unpredictable currents that sweep around this headland and take care if paddling in the shallows as there can be a surprisingly strong undertow – but otherwise enjoy the wild and generally deserted environment. In bygone days, before the lighthouse was built, pilgrims would come here to ritually cleanse themselves. The blood, sweat and tears

that you may have shed along the way are part of our individual and collective purification. Fire and water were also associated with purification and rebirth.

An ancient rite, followed by some modern pilgrims, involved burning one's old clothes and donning fresh garments as an act of renewal. Recycling, rather than burning, might be an environmentally responsible modification. An endearing ritual here also involved kneeling (not swimming) in the shallows and allowing nine waves to wash over the body – representing a rebirth into a new life washed clean by spirit. No one needs permission to devise their own rituals provided their focus is love and they are performed discreetly and safely with due respect to the traditional environment in which they are offered. Pilgrims now mostly come here to simply celebrate life in this beautiful spot away from the crowds.

From here there are several ways back to the town centre and pilgrim hostels. *[**Note:** the routes are not well waymarked but the town location is obvious].* The most direct route is via the hamlet of **A Insua** (now effectively a suburb of Finisterre). Make your way back along the path you originally came down but carry s/o at the first turning (now on your right) [0.3 km] and follow the path s/o up to the asphalt road and turn right> [0.2 km] and <left at T-junction [0.2 km] *(Hotel Rústico Ínsua right)* and take the road all the way down to main roundabout by Hotel Ancora and the primary school [0.5 km] and s/o down to the town centre [0.2 km]. *(An alt. path leads past the sport hall deportivo to the Arenal / Baixamar district at the north end of town – see map).*

Finisterre's symbolic significance and potency is not lost on the pilgrims who continue to come here seeking to reconcile the conflict of inner and outer realities in their lives. This guidebook seeks, however inadequately, to find a balance between these 'outer' and 'inner' worlds and the following notes relate to the fascinating culture of Galicia and the mythology and significance of Finisterre as both a modern and ancient pilgrim destination. The following legendary sites are marked on the map of Cabo Finisterre so you can readily identify them.

The *Ara Solis* and the sacred stones *Piedras Santas* became natural altars for the ancient rites where the 'world of things and the world of spirits' met. Such was the significance of this site, that the Romans built here the legendary city of Dugium *(Dugio /Duyo /Duio)*. It is said that legionnaires retired here to end their days where they were closest to the 'meeting of the worlds' and paradise itself. This is, perhaps, a reference to the Elysian Fields mentioned by the Roman historian Estrabon as, 'a peaceful place, where once dead heroes and those favoured by the gods found rest... a place in the far west, at the confines of the earth, where the sun hid.' Benjamín Trillo Trillo in *As Pegadas de Santiago na Cultura de Fisterra* goes further suggesting that Finisterre was the original and favoured place for the burial of St. James:

> *The route of Saint James is in reality the route of the west, the one followed by the sun on its way to sunset [where] the mansion of pious souls can be found... We cannot forget the explicit naming of the town of Duio in the Liber Sancti Jacobi, nor that the king of the town prevented the disciples of Saint James from burying his body in the surroundings of Fisterra. For this reason we can understand perfectly why the pilgrims, who for many centuries went to the town of Compostela, would also want to visit Fisterra, in order to see among other things the place where the body of the apostle should have been buried if the devil had not prevented it.*

Thankfully, little remains to authenticate the historical origins of Duio and so it lives on in legend far more forcefully than if it were just another tourist site. It seems the early Christian Church sought out the sacred sites of pagans and Druids in order to graft its own message directly onto these cultures. Any area that held spiritual significance was the logical place to endeavour to weave a new consciousness. It is therefore entirely reasonable to assume that Saint James would have come *specifically* to Finisterre as one of the foremost sites of spiritual practise and ritual in the then known world. More speculative is the notion that he may, in turn, have been following in the footsteps of his Master.

Legends abound of Jesus travelling with Joseph of Aramathea to visit Druidic teachers in Cornwall. It has already been suggested that Joseph earned his wealth from trading in tin and importing it to Palestine from the mines in Britannia. The Phoenicians and Romans had opened a sea route between the two countries the previous century and this route went directly past the Roman seaport of *Artabrorum Portus* mentioned by Ptolemy and described as, 'a large port serving an intense trading activity,' that scholars have identified as Finisterre. This is corroborated by the writings of George Borrow who described the port as, "echoing with a thousand voices when the ships and trade of all known lands met in Duio." There is general agreement that the present day hamlet of San Martiño de Duio is the Duio referred to and this in turn derives from the Roman town of Dugium built on the site of a former Celtic Citania here.

❹ ● **Christ of the Golden Beard** *Cristo da Barba Dourada.* If Jesus
travelled to Britannia during the 18 years when we know nothing of his whereabouts it would be reasonable to assume that his ship would have gone ashore on this stretch of coast for provisions. In such a case it would be inconceivable that Jesus did not meet with the Druidic masters who served this most important centre of
spiritual initiation. It is interesting that the figure of Jesus continues to play such an important part in the customs of modern day Finisterre. Miracles have always been associated with the remarkably beautiful effigy of Christ on the Cross that hangs in the ancient parish Church of Santa Maria. This image is said to have been created by Nicodemus who, along with Joseph of Aramathea prepared the body of Jesus for burial. This beautiful figure known and revered as 'The Christ of the Golden Beard' *Cristo da Barba Dourada* has long been associated with miraculous powers of healing and it was believed that the body perspired and the beard was seen to grow. How this statue came to reside in Finisterre has become a legend in itself. A ship sailing to England encountered a storm while passing Finisterre and would have foundered had not the crew thrown the figure of Christ into the waters whereupon the sea became miraculously calmed.

The highlight of the religious calendar in Finisterre is Holy Week celebrated each year with a moving re-enactment of Christ's death, burial and resurrection when a white dove is released symbolising the Holy Spirit ascending into heaven. This annual festival draws thousands of people from all over Spain and is designated of national importance.

● **The Wine Stained Rock** *Piedra Manchada de Vino.* The relatively inaccessible cove of **Cabanas** faces east towards Monte Pindo and here we find another of the legends associating Christ with Finisterre. Jesus is said to have appeared at this spot to hold back the waters threatening to submerge the town. It was also here that San Guillerme (whose hermitage lies above the road at this point) met with sailors who gave him a barrel of wine that he tried to carry back up the steep slope. The devil, disguised as a peasant, offered to help but dragged him backwards smashing the cask on the rocks below which became red – birthing the legend of the wine-stained rock *piedra manchada de vino.* This is also the place where the figure of Christ and his statue were said to have been washed ashore. Above the site is the modern burial ground *cementerio (casa de todos los muertos).*

The legends surrounding St. James give wonderfully descriptive portrayals of his death and burial in Galicia. But few direct their attention to why he came initially to Galicia to preach and why his body was returned to an obscure area known as Libredon. Padrón is popularly identified as the town where he first set foot in Galicia to preach the gospel and to which his body was returned for burial. We have already seen that Finisterre was one of the most powerful places of ancient worship and spiritual initiation in the known-world and it lies a mere days sail from Padrón and 3 days walk from Santiago. Those tenuous threads that link Jesus with Finisterre become much stronger in linking St. James with this headland. While Padrón was well established as a trading port so was Dugium which, in addition, had the essential spiritual significance making it the ideal and logical destination.

❺ **Lighthouse** *Faro* ● **Peace Pole & Fire-Pit.** Owing to its pagan past Finisterre has been largely excluded from the Santiago story. But this exclusion has allowed Finisterre the freedom to become a beacon of light to welcome all people in its universal embrace. This inclusivity is evidenced by the planting of one of the first Peace Poles in Spain into the solid rock of Cabo Finisterre. This internationally recognised symbol of the hopes and dreams of the entire human family stands vigil in silent prayer for universal peace and adjoins the lighthouse. Finisterre has always been a link between east and west – between inner and outer authority. The Way to Finisterre affords us an opportunity to let go out-worn belief systems based on fear, guilt and separation. Once we have dispensed with limiting prejudice and dogma we become open and

ready to receive a new wisdom based on inclusivity and cooperation. So here, behind the lighthouse, an ancient pilgrim rite has been revived. The local council has provided a fire-pit so that pilgrims can burn an item of old clothing or other token to represent the letting-go of the old in order to awaken to the new. Remember this is a symbolic gesture and doesn't require the burning of an entire wardrobe! An old sock or a simple handwritten note will do perfectly.

Having played its part in the establishment of Christianity in Europe, acting as a magnet for the first Christian missionaries, Finisterre may yet have a role in the unfolding of a new epoch – one less dependent on the idea of a 'chosen people' and embracing all humanity. The desire for specialness based on exclusion has been the greatest cause of war and suffering in the human story. Until we focus on what connects us rather than what divides us we will never find lasting peace in our world. From the Human Rights movement sprang the phrase, *All men and women are created equal* but we have yet to find the courage to live out that noble truth. Perhaps the path to the 'end of the way and the world' will yet become a starting point for a new consciousness based on unconditional love of God, neighbour and self.

❻ ● Hermitage of Saint William
Ermita de San Guillerme. This 5th C hermitage is located on a site that St. James himself is said to have preached from in his attempt to discredit the pagan rituals practised at the nearby *Ara Solis*. This is easier to understand if we remember that the Christ Light, with its promise of a New Jerusalem, arose in the east. Trillo Trillo states:

> *The hermitage, associated both with Saint James and the Ara Solis, was the ideal place to find Christ in the Middle Ages [and] there is a clear relationship between the Hermitage of San Guillerme and the Resurrection of Christ in the Christian tradition: the heathens believed in the fertility powers of the Ara Solis whilst the Christians believed in the saving grace of Christ. Immortality is not achieved through reproduction, but by the resurrection.*

But it is also clear that the lines between paganism and Christianity are often smudged. San Guillerme's 'bed' a stone plinth with its shallow depression has long been associated with miraculous powers of fertility and drew infertile couples to 'lie together' on its surface in their desire to conceive, aided by the powers of the saint himself. Ancient fertility rites have long been associated

with this headland. There is also some confusion as to whom San Guillerme actually was. Some sources suggest he was none other than Saint Guillerme le Désert the French hermit who founded the pilgrimage centre on the Arles camino built around a fragment of the True Cross. Perhaps most understood him simply as a holy man who lived a devout life based on Christ's teaching. Above the hermitage, at the top of the Monte de San Guillerme, is one of several sites associated with the Ara Solis. Wherever its exact position it is clear that all pagan altars will have been systematically destroyed by the newly emerging Christian religion.

❼ ● **Monte Facho** *Ara Solis:* The first references to the Sun Temple *Ara Solis* came from the Romans who, when they arrived here in the 1ˢᵗ century BC, came across the Phoenician altar and witnessed a thriving place of worship and spiritual initiation. While there is some difference in opinion as to the exact location of 'the' altar to some extent the entire headland must have acted as a sacred site and would have been used in its entirety in ceremonial processions and worship. Whatever of the pagan rites practised here over the centuries one (Christian) interpretation is that the horizon represented the lip of the Chalice, a symbol of the Holy Grail itself, and the sun represented the Host – a symbolic representation that forms the emblem of Galicia today *(see image and also Galician flag p.13)* which incorporates a chalice with host above it surrounded by seven crosses representing the seven historical cities of Galicia. The highest spot on the headland was inevitably a place of major significance. It is here that we find the Holy

Stones **Piedras Santas** and a location for the **Ara Solis** with access opposite the *Piedra del Carballo de Oro*. Perhaps you will be able to locate the Rocking Stone *Abalar* and have the experience of moving 10 tons of solid granite with your own hand, *"If ye have faith as a grain of mustard seed, ye shall say to this mountain, move hence to yonder place; and it shall move and nothing shall be impossible unto you."* [*The photo top is taken from the Piedras Santas and shows the* **Cabo Da Nave** *(circled) said to represent a Roman Centurion laid to rest with his helmeted head facing west to the 'Land of Eternal Youth'*].

A Christian myth tells of the Virgin Mary resting over these stones but pagan worshippers had a very different interpretation. Here we can see how a prior pagan initiation rite was erased from popular memory by the substitution of a new Christian legend. It is said the Virgin appeared here to encourage St. James in his ministry. But it is not generally known that these stones are easily moved *abalar* and were allegedly the site of an earlier pagan rite whereby the movement of the stones proved (or disproved) the virginity of a priestess before she was allowed to perform certain ceremonial duties. The phrase 'to put her over the stone' was a reference to this ordeal. What better way to extinguish such references to this ancient practise but by instigating a new legend whereby the Virgin Mary appeared in this selfsame spot to support the ministry of St. James. A parallel pagan practise and similar substitution took place at Muxía (see later).

The small island just offshore to the south/west is named after the Spider Crab *Centola* found at Finisterre and associated with the abode of the devil. The Christian church often promulgated fearful myths of devil worship associated with paganism in order to frighten superstitious locals from cavorting with the heathens. One such classic tale relates to the witch Orcavella who is said to have seduced unwary young men into her snake-ridden cave and 'smothered' them to death with her embrace. Just in case the younger generation should show interest in these pagan rituals – she was known to eat children as well. Further exploration is discouraged as her cave is said to lie behind the fence surrounding the wireless station.

● **Orcavella's Tomb** *Tomba de Orcavella*. There are several sources that relate the legend of the witch Orcavella who lived in a cave on Monte Facho. The following is a shortened extract from *O Camiño de Fisterra* by Fernando Alonso Romero and refers to the *Silva Curiosa* published in Paris in 1583 wherein the knight Medrano describes his pilgrimage to Fisterra and the story told him by a hermit there. This hermit described the existence of an ancient sepulchre 'in a deserted and isolated place near which were some large high rocks'. The knight went to investigate and as he approached the place a shepherd came running and shouting:

> *Keep away! Good Lord, brother, where are you going? Do you want to perish? Amongst those rocks there is enclosed the damned body of the enchantress Orcabella. Every man or woman who has set eyes upon her has died within a year. She could make herself invisible and robbed and ate as many children she had a mind to... and left half the kingdom depopulated. When she got tired of living, she withdrew to these crags and in one of them she carved out her tomb. With the help of a shepherd whom she kept a spellbound prisoner, she raised up a big tombstone to cover the sepulchre and slid it on the opening to cover it. Afterwards she undressed and embracing the sad shepherd she threw him into the sepulchre and shut him in there. Leaving her clothes outside, got into this deadly bed, and using the unfortunate shepherd as a mattress, lay on top of him. The unlucky shepherd shouted and screamed so much that other shepherds who were in that bleak place, ran to where the shouts came from and were surprised and frightened to see that the sepulchre was completely surrounded by snakes and serpents.*

● **Dugium** *San Martino de Duio* There is nothing to actually 'see' of Dugium and only limited archaeological investigations have taken place in the area. Despite this Trillo Trillo cites Aldao Carré noting that Dugium was no myth and that the remains of dwellings as well as objects from flint axe heads to brick pavements and Roman pottery are evidence of this. The legendary site of ***Dugium (Duio)*** lies [2.3 km] North of Finisterre on the path to Muxía so if you are continuing on that route you pass right through the area. This route also passes the turning to **Hermedesuxo** *The Site* of an intriguing hypothesis put forward by the knowledgeable Trillo Trillo as follows:

> *The existence of such a city ... begs the question: Who was or were the religious deities who protected it? Hermes was the god of traders and also had links with the fertility myth. I mention [this] link because there is a place called Hermedesujo in the valley of Duio. In a XIIth Century document... Hermedesujo de Abajo appears as 'Hermo'... Although*

the usual linguistic interpretation of the word Hermo would be 'an uninhabitable place', such an explanation does not fit with the facts. And it is for this reason that one should not rule out the possibility this place, once called Hermes was later turned into Hermo owing to Christianity's eagerness to demystify local place names. Murguía adds: 'Let us not forget the pyschopompic Hermes [was also] the soul bearer.

Continuing the ever popular theme of death and dying is the ominous name given to this entire coastline – **Coast of Death** *Costa da Morte* a reference, perhaps, to the cult of the dead or the Celtic Otherworld than to its manifold shipwrecks. Due west of Duio lies Ship Headland *Cabo de Nave* with its allusion to the boat that carries the souls of the dead to the Underworld ruled over by Hades. The headland here together with the small island directly off it *Berrón da Nave* looks like a helmeted Roman soldier (when viewed from Monte Facho) – his body laid to rest with his head lying to the west.

It is, perhaps, a pity that factual records of these pagan, Phoenician, Celtic and Roman rites have been largely erased from the history books. The early Christian church, no doubt threatened by the ideas behind worship of the sun and the notion of *Tir-na-Nóg*, suppressed what information was available. Today we can only marvel at the zeal of early pilgrims, Christian and pre-Christian, that risked life and limb to travel to this remote corner of the Earth. It is likely that interest in this legendary headland will draw ever-increasing numbers to visit. It is important to respect the sacred nature of this landscape and to keep the area free of litter and celebration parties – let's keep the wine and beer to the bar or beach and don't let irritation at disrespectful behaviour allow us to leave behind the psychic rubbish of superiority or resentment!

We would do well to remember that our rituals are symbolic of some greater understanding and the most important thing is to find a place where we can feel at peace to connect to that deeper wisdom. The actual rock or earth upon which we carry out our chosen ritual, prayer or meditation is immaterial – it is the energy of love that makes the ceremony sacred, not the place. The mystical notes from stage one cautioned us not to confuse sacred sites with insight and A Course In Miracles reminds us that the true temple is not a structure at all – its holiness lies at the inner altar whose beauty cannot be seen with the physical eye. An emphasis on beautiful structures can be a sign of unwillingness to exercise spiritual vision.

Countless thousands have travelled to Finisterre over millennia as witness to some force beyond our understanding. Overlooking the harbour at the end of our journey is the haunting monument to the emigrant. As we arrive at the end of the world it is perhaps humbling to recall the thousands that departed from this selfsame spot to start their own journey of discovery of a brave 'New World.'

... it was late in the day, as I came down the hill from the Ara Solis, when an otherworldly luminescence appeared out of the gloom. It had rained incessantly for 10 days and now on the last day the sun was beginning to break through. I became aware of a butterfly hovering above the path and tears started to fall – I had emerged from my own chrysalis and in that moment knew it was not the outer journey but the inner focus that would be the new basis for my life. I write these notes from a balcony looking east over Monte Pindo. A Course In Miracles lies open to remind me that, "   All my past, except its beauty, is gone and nothing is left but a blessing."

We shall not cease from exploration
And the end of all our exploring
Will be to arrive where we started
And know the place for the first time.

Four Quartets, *T.S. Eliot*

4 FINISTERRE – MUXÍA

░░░░░░░░░	--- ---	13.7	--- ---	49%
────────	--- ---	14.4	--- ---	51%
────────	--- ---	0.0	--- ---	0%
Total km		**28.1 km (17.5 ml)**		

▲▲ Total Ascent **540** m ± *54 mins*
*Alto.*m ▲ Monte Lourido **270**m *(885 ft)*
< Ⓐ Ⓗ > ➲Lires **13.5** km ➲Frixe **15.5** km

Walk slow, don't rush. That place you have to reach is yourSelf
José Ortega y Gasset.

The Practical Path: Delightful forest paths and farm tracks offer shade and shelter from the unpredictable weather along this remote Atlantic coast where the sea is never far away and often clearly visible. This stage to Muxía is becoming justifiably popular but still provides a sense of adventure. Around halfway we dip down into the beautiful Lires estuary that offers the only reasonably safe place for a swim and an opportunity for a midday break in the cafés... or stay the night? (Note: if you plan to stay in the Xunta hostel in Muxía you need to collect a stamp *sello* here).

0.0 km Centro From municipal albergue ❸ in the centre of Finisterre head up c/ Santa Catalina past Concello and s/o at the junction with main road to **Cruz de Baximar [0.4** km] *[for alt. 'green' route to San Salvador via Praia de Langosteira turn down right and continue along beach path and turn up left via carpark at bar Trebón [1.2 km] s/o over main road at café Alberto to join waymarked route [0.4 km].* For main waymarked continue s/o and urn up <left at •**Hotel Arenal** by the corner with ☕ *San Roque* **[0.7** km]

1.1 km Arenal *sign* **San Martiño de Duio** and first <Fisterra – Muxía> waymark. Head uphill and veer right> **[0.4** km] where the road levels off to pass **San Martiño de Duio parish church [0.4** km] and continue along the side of the Duio valley (site of the legendary city of Dugium) with fine sea views and turn up <left at **Escaselas crossroads [1.2** km] *[alt. 'green' route joins from right]* through **Hermedesuxo [0.5** km] to **crossroads [0.2** km] and take the road signposted **San Salvador [0.4** km].

3.1 km San Salvador •*Hr*¨**Dugium** ✆ 606 606 480 currently only available as entire house <u>www.dugium.com</u> Continue s/o up into pine forest around **alto Rapadoira**, down into **Rial** and:

✠ *Santuario da Virxe de Barca*

4 A ← **1.0** **Centro**
MUXÍA *(Pop. 4,800)*

Opción **2.2**

✠ San Roque
Monasterio Moraime
A *S. Xulián*
P *Paris*
Os Muiños

Praia Lourido
≋ *Vista*

Parador Spa **H**

2.5 **Opción**

Xurarantes

Monte Lourido
310m ▲
270m
Alto ← **3.0** **Alto**

Cabo Touriñan

Viseo

3.9 **Morquintián**
Fuente / Cruceiro

Vilachán

Touriñan

O Muiño
Guisamonde

Alemán +1.4 km ⊡

Nemiña

Frixe Abaixo
Frixe **2.0** **C** *Casa Ceferinos*
Kiosco
Pontenova

río Castro
Praia de Nemiña
A Braña
Cabanas
3.6 **C** **2.5** **Lires**
Playa **A** *As Eiras*
Porcar

río Lires

Opción **4.2**
Canosa

Praia de Rostro

Padrís

Castrexe

A **2.6** **Buxán**
Sinfín
Rial

Castromiñán

Dugíum
H **3.1** **San Salvador**
Castro
Mallas
Hermedesuxo
Anchoa
C-552
Cee

Corcubión

río Lires

Duio
San Martiño
✠ *Trebol*
Arenal ← **1.1**
Arenal **H**
Baixamar

Praia de Langosteira

Praia de Mar do Fora

Lires **13.5 km** – – *Xunta* **Centro 0.0** **3 A**
(Pop. 4,700)
FINISTERRE

O – E
Sunset *Sunrise*
S

CAMINO
GUIDES.COM

2.6 km **Buxán** •*Alb.* **Sinfin** ✆ 609 041 590 with fine views over the coast where Marta & Jose Luis may provide a pilgrim rest area and possible floorspace to overnight. Turn down <left and imm. right> out of the village past timber yard and continue on asphalt road to next group of houses at **Suarriba** with the wild coast now clearly visible and turn <left [!] down wide track towards village below. **Castrexe** small hamlet and nearest point to Rostro beach. *Note: if you want to visit one of the remotest beaches in Galicia it is only 400 meters. Do NOT swim here as this coast can be very dangerous [!].* To continue to Muxía turn right> out of Castrexe and take the first track <left and then right> at asphalt up into **Padrís** and veer <left onto delightful track through pine and eucalyptus woods to option point:

4.2 km **Opción*** The route is officially waymarked via **Canosa** but if the weather is reasonable and you have time (+ ½ hour) the beautiful alternative option along the Lires estuary is recommended – adding just 1.1 km.

For alt. coastal route ● ● ● ● *[3.6 km -v- main route 2.5 km]* veer <left along woodland path that winds down to join forestry track with fine views of the beautiful coastline to the west. The path leads down onto quiet asphalt road at the estuary of río Lires with sandy beach that the locals use for swimming and ⑪ Tapas Bar Playa (summer). *(If you intend to swim*

beware of changing tidal flows and river currents at any time of year – watch where the locals swim!). Fishermen often line both banks of the estuary here with fish feeding off the local fish farm effluent. The route follows the road around the estuary to cross over the bridge and join up with the main route at the church of Saint Stephen *San Esteban* at the entrance to Lires.

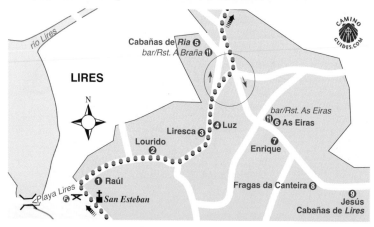

For the main route continue s/o (right) at *option** point down to concrete lane through **Canosa** and turn left alongside the rego da Carbaliza to join asphalt road into **Lires** at Iglesia San Esteban *Igrexa San estebo* with view of the *Ría de Lires* and the *Praia de Nemiña* where the alternative route joins from the left. Turn right up into village:

2.5 km **Lires** ❖ crossroads & option to take a break or overnight in this delightful village overlooking the Lires estuary with good facilites incl. ❶*CR* **Raúl** *x4* €40-50 © 981 748 156 ❷*CR Lourido x7* €35-45 © 981 748 203 ❸*H* **Liresca** *Lires on the Camino x10* €40-50 © 981 464 395 *www.liresca. com* ❹*P*''**Casa Luz** *x5* €35-45 © 981 748 924. ❺**Cabañas** *de Ria x3* €100+ (2 sharing) © 981 748 393 upmarket timber chalets and tipis from €25pp with ¶*Vbar A Braña* on terrace overlooking the estuary (photo>) *[Part of Ecoturismo Lires who also operate CR Jesus].* **Centre of Lires:**

❻*Alb.*& *P*'''**As Eiras** *Priv.[23÷4]* €15 © 981 748 180 (Pablo) m: 662 261 818 (photo>) *www.ruralaseiras.com* popular *Bar/* ¶ and bikes to explore nearby beaches. ❼*Apt.* **Casa Enrique** *x2* €60 © 981 748 170. ❽*P*''**Fragas da Canteira** *x10* €40-60 © 981 748 997 *www.fragasdacanteira.com* ❾*CR*

Jesús *x6* €30-50 © 696 029 810 + adj. **Cabañas** *de Lires x3 cabins* €80+ © 981 748 393 with swimpool & gardens.

To continue turn <left at crossroads ❖ and veer right onto forest track down to a tributary of the **río Castro**. A new concrete bridge now satisfies the health and safety executive but eliminates the last 'funky' crossing via the original stepping stones still visible downstream. Cross river and head up track by **Bau Silbeiro** and continue s/o (an alternative route goes by the asphalt road right) veer right into woods to rejoin road and continue into **Frixe**.

2.0 km **Frixe** ⬥ *Drink Kiosk* & w.c. *[right* off *route for* •*CR* **Ceferinos** *x10* €35+ © 981 748 965 *Lugar de Frixe Nº15 +½ km].* Turn up onto path crossing over the **Touriñán road** *[The lighthouse at Cabo Touriñan is the most westerly point in Spain + 7.5 km 'O Último Sol', café Alemán + 1.4 km].* Turn **down** <left and imm. right> by farm building to crossroads at **Guisamonde** ⬥ *O Muiño* s/o into **Morquintián**.

3.9 km **Morquintián** drinking font by *cruceiro*. Keep s/o and veer right up past houses and continue to **T-Junction** and turn right> [!] *(not the original waymarked route left)* and then take path <left up into woods. This next stretch is a delightful path that winds its way around the gorse-strewn slopes

of **As Aferroas** and **Monte Facho de Lourido** with views over the Ría de Camariñas climbing gently towards today's high point *Alto (270m)*.

3.0 km **Alto** the track now begins a gentle descent but zig zags down through the woodland so stay alert for waymarks into the village of **Xurarantes.** Turn <left and then right> down asphalt road passing fountain **Fuente** (left – with cool waters favoured by the locals) to T-junction and option point:

2.5 km Road *Option:* The waymarked route turns right along the asphalt road all the way into **Muxía** *or...* continue s/o over new road to parador and onto path for short and delightful detour over the sand dunes around **Praia de Lourido.** There are too many paths here to be specific but make your way down towards the beach onto the sandy headland. At this point make your way to the right over tidal mud flats to take the wide track back up to the main road visible above with view point **Punta de Vista** on the main road above Praia de Lourido. The new build on the headland (see photo>) is the latest Parador •*H*···**Costa da Morte** *x62* €110+ © 881 161 111. From here we follow the road along a bleak stretch of rocky coast past the town football ground to the Southern outskirts of Muxía.

2.2 km Muxía *option* The town is a maze of narrow streets so decide where you are heading at the entrance to the town ❖ (see town plan):

Ⓐ Take road up right direct to the Xunta hostel [**0.7** km] or Ⓑ keep s/o to the town centre, pilgrim office and central hostels [**1.0** km] or Ⓒ Take the left (seaward) road direct to the *Sanctuario de Virxe da Barca* [**1.5** km].

❖ Ⓐ Take the 'back' road direct to the Xunta hostel [**0.7** km]. Turn up right> at the option (imm. past house no: 45 at the entrance to Muxía) to T-junction and turn up right> into **rúa Os Malatos** [**0.2** km] past Guardia Civil to top of road which curves to the left and continue to T-junction [**0.5** km] and *Alb.* Ⓢ **Xunta** [32÷2] €8 ultra-modern concrete building at the top of rúa Enfesto at the southern side of town with good modern facilities in utilitarian style building with large reception area.

❖ Ⓑ S/o [**0.2** km] to ❶ **Da Costa** *Priv.*[8÷1] €15 *+1* €45 © 676 363 820 (Silvia y Carlos) c/Doctor Toba, 33. ❷ **Muxía Mare** *Priv.*[16÷2] €14 *+2* €40 © 981 742 423 r/Castelao, 14. S/o to **Coido** [**0.2** km] (park gets setting sun) and next option.

❖ Ⓒ [to go direct to Sanctuario de Virxe da Barca veer left by coast into rúa Coido into rúa Atalaia (avoiding cul-de-sacs to the left) to the sanctuary [**1.5** km].

To continue to town centre ❖ ❸ keep s/o via r/Areal into José Maria del Rio N°30 ❸ **Arribada** *Priv.*[40÷4] €15 +*4* €50+ Ⓒ 981 742 516 or veer right into **Rúa Real** [**0.3** km] (corner r/Real & r/Eduardo Pondal •*P*''' **Hábitat** *CM x14* €40-50 Ⓒ 981 742 148. Turn <left up the main street past •*P* **Alemana** *x4* €60+ Ⓒ 986 064 877 with popular wine bar 🍴 *Vinoteca* r/ Virxe da Barca, 3. Adj. •*P* **Pedra D'Abalar** *x6* €30 Ⓒ 981 742 063 (adj. 🍴 *bar Prestige*) into small plaza [**0.2** km] with •*H*'' **A de Loló** *x4* €39-59 Ⓒ 981

742 422 *www.adelolo.com* modern boutique hotel (see photo>) close to ultra modern ❹ **Bela Muxía** [**44÷4**] €15 +*16* €40-65 Ⓒ 687 798 222 (Ángel Castro) *www.belamuxia.com* welcoming central pension/alb. with all facilities and terraces overlooking the harbour on r/Encarnación, 30. Note the entrance is *behind* the central tourist office 100 m further [**0.1** km].

`1.0 km` **Muxía** *Centro* ❶ *Turismo* in the *Casa Cultura* rúa Virxe da Barca,

47 Ⓒ 981 742 563. The tourist office is also a pilgrim information centre and issues the **Muxíanna**, modelled on the *Fisterrana* and the *Compostela*, to pilgrims who have walked to Muxía from Santiago on presentation of a stamped credencial. In the event the office is closed albergue Bela Muxía to the rear is also licensed to issue the Muxíana and keeps detailed information on bus schedules etc and has a bank of computers for internet searches.

Other Lodging *Central*: ❻ @Muxía *Priv.*[40÷2] €15 Ⓒ 609 615 533 *www.albergueamuxia.com* c/Enfesto, 12 below the Xunta hostel. *[Note: Hungarian Alb.* **Delphin** *on the seafront is now closed]*. Back on rua Real 52 •*P* **Casa Isolina** *x5* Ⓒ 981 742 367 €25+ m: 630 581 744 (family operate *Bar Wimpe* on the harbour front). On the eastern entrance/exit is •*Hs*'' **La Cruz** *x30* €40-45 Ⓒ 981 742 084 Av. López Avente, 44. **Outside town:** •*P*' **O Rincón da Baiuca** *x7* €65 Ⓒ 981 742 583 Largo da Baiuca (+0.7 km from La Cruz): See also next stage for albergue **Monasterio de Moraime** (+3.2 km). Note: A number of private houses may also offer lodging (look for signs on windows) and apartments are also available. One of the more central is: •*Apts.* **A Bughina** Ⓒ 679 796 042 on r/Virxe da Barca, 1.

🍴*Restaurants / bars* around the harbour area: Note these restaurants face east and do not get the evening sun (see town plan). *O Porto – A Pedra d'Abalar – Wimpe – A Marina –* Towards La Cruz *Casa do Peixe – O Xardín menú*.

Return to Santiago: *Ferrin Grupo* © 981 873 643 <u>*www.grupoferrin.com*</u>
Twice daily 06:45 & 14:30 (later on Sunday) check schedule at bus-stop on
rúa Marina. Bus takes around 1¼ hours). *Taxi* © 981 742 070 Santiago (±
1 hour) ± €90.

Muxía: Fishing port with a
population of 5,200 that has made the
most of the poor economic climate
that has blighted much of rural
Galicia. Despite the harsh Atlantic
weather that beats against its shores
it looks brighter now than it did
some years ago. Houses have been
renovated, the college upgraded and 4
new pilgrim hostels completed. Apart
from summer tourism the mainstay of
the town has been the modern fishing fleet that hums with activity from the
rich fishing grounds offshore. A walk around the harbour and through the
old town will acquaint you with an authentic Galician fishing village. It is
delightfully easy to get lost in the narrow streets that run between rúa Atalaia
on the west and rúas Real and Virxe da Barca to the east – use the sun to
orientate yourself or enjoy the 'lostness'. The name Muxía is derived from
Mongía land of monks from the nearby 12thC Romanesque monastic church
San Xulián de Moraime. These monks came here in 1105 in an effort to
suppress the pagan rituals that were being practised at that time (see stage 5).

Muxía's is connected to the Santiago
story through the legend of **Our Lady
of the Boat** *Nosa Señora da Barca*
and the Sanctuary at the headland
Santuario da Virxe da Barca located
at the far end of town (due North).
A popular pilgrimage site in its own
right and associated with the Virgin
Mary who, the legend claims, came
here in a boat made of stone to help
St. James in his ministry. St. James, feeling that he had failed in his mission to
convert the population of Finisterre from their worship of the sun, travelled
to this remote place for rest and succour. As he prayed he saw a boat with the
Virgin Mary aboard, 'full of mystery and majesty', approaching the headland.
The Virgin assured him that his ministry had in fact been successful and that
his work here was done and he should return to Jerusalem.

The legend tells us that the boat in which she travelled became petrified
in the stones we see here on the headland. The most obvious is the stone
sail *Pedra dos Cadris* (see photo>) which reputedly has miraculous powers
of healing – pass under the stone 9 times to be cured of rheumatism and

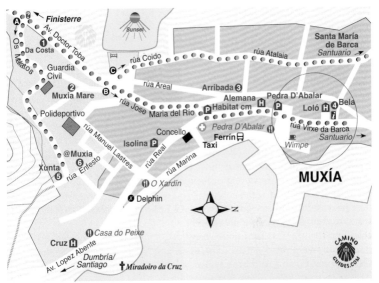

associated ailments. The rudder stone *Pedra do Timón* and rocking hull *Pedra da Abalar* are nearby. This latter stone moves on its axis and was used to prove innocence or guilt of any accused brought before it. It was cracked during a storm in 1978 but its powers of attraction remain undiminished. Also nearby is the lovers' stone *Pedra dos Namorados* where couples come to pledge their love.

Watching over all this activity is the austere 18th century sanctuary dedicated to the Virgin. Originally founded in the 12th century on a pre-Christian site. It was hit by a lightening strike on Christmas day 2013 and severely damaged by the ensuing fire but has been rebuilt. You can approach it either via option **C** (page 74) known as the Way of the Skin *Camiño da Pel.* So called because a fountain here was used by pilgrims to wash and purify themselves before entering the sanctuary *or* via rúa Marina along the harbour front. Both routes are 1.5 km (0.7 km from the tourist office). Just above the sanctuary is the split stone monument ***A Ferida*** *La Herida* (The Wound – see photo previous page.) a reminder of the oil spill from the tanker Prestige which led to the movement 'Never Again' *Nunca Mais.* Here we find another smaller paved path that goes to the top of the conical hillock *Monte Corpiño* 81 metres high and a 400m climb to the 360° view of the town, the harbour, and the hamlet of *Chorente* on the wooded headland due south through which the path continues to Dumbria (stage 5). From here there is also a distant view north/east across the bay to the village of *Camariñas* famous for its fine handmade lace (see photo>). Bus every 3 hours journey time ½ hour cost €5. Taxi €35 (25 km).

To return to the town centre take the rúa Virxe da Barca that connects the sanctuary with the town centre and harbour area. Along this way is the 14th century parish church of Saint Mary *Iglesia de Santa Maria* built in the coastal-Gothic style *gótica-marinero*. A major pilgrimage *Romaría da Virxe da Barca* takes place every year in September.

At the western end of town (setting sun) are the rails for drying the conger eels *Secadero de Congrios* a delicacy in Galicia (see photo>). This remains the only place still sun drying conger by this method *https://concellomuxia. com/en/item/secadoiro-dos-cascons/* The main fishing activity is centred around the fish market *Lonxa* in the port area which has murals and photos

of the sinking of the Prestige. Most of the catch now goes to be sold at the fish market in A Coruña. A wide variety of fish is landed here from the rich fishing grounds offshore and up until recently Muxia ranked as the leading hake fishing port in Spain.

REFLECTIONS:

Muxía harbour front from miradoiro de cruz

5 MUXÍA – OLVEIROA *via DUMBRIA*

....	--- ---	15.9	--- ---	49%
▬▬▬	--- ---	16.4	--- ---	51%
▬▬▬	--- ---	0.0	--- ---	0%
Total km		**32.3** km *(20.1 ml)*		

Total Ascent **850** m ± *85 mins*

Alto.m ▲ Hospital 385 m *(1,263 ft)*

< Ⓐ Ⓗ > ●Os Muinos **5.2** km ●Ozón **9.4**
●Quintáns **10.8** ●A Grixa **15.3** ●Dumbría
21.8 ●Hospital **27.4** ●Logoso **28.8** km.

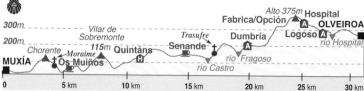

Life must be lived forwards, but can only be understood backwards.
Kierkegaard

The Practical Path: A long stage but ½ is on forest tracks providing shelter and new interim hostels give options to break the journey. The route is not so clearly waymarked in this clockwise direction so extra vigilance is required. Use the sun-compass to help with orientation and beware of arrows in the *opposite* direction pointing back to Muxia. Take water and snacks and allow time to retrace steps if necessary.

0.0 km Centro from the town centre *Alb.*❹ **Bela Muxía** head south along Rúa Mariña past Miradoiro da Cruz and turn <left onto a board-walk that skirts the edge of the *praia Espiñeirido* cross s/o road at far end onto **woodland path [1.6 km]** and up steeply through woods around *Monte de Chorente* with views back over Muxía and the wide bay *Ría*

Camariñas and *Cabo Vilán*. Continue along walled lane to the village of **Chorente [1.0** km] veer right> then up <left to our high point of this section at the chapel of Saint Roch **[0.6** km].

3.2 km **Capela de San Roque** – pleasant woodland rest area with cruceiro. Head downhill over main road and turn right> and imm. <left downhill past ancient *fonte* and 🍴 *tapas bar* opposite the Romanesque church of St. Julian

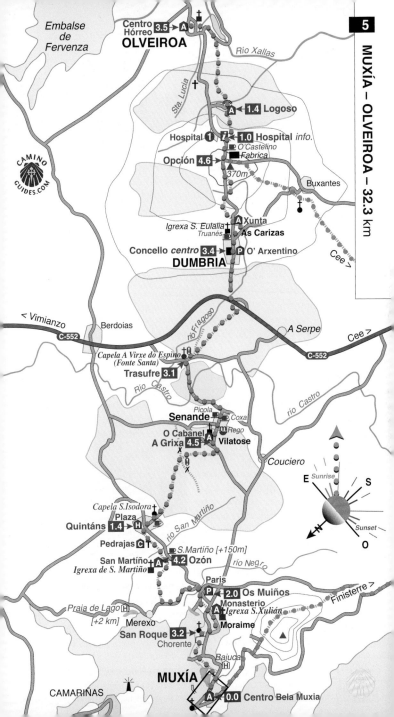

Embalse de Fervenza

Centro Hórreo `3.5` Ⓐ
OLVEIROA

Río Xallas

Sta. Lucía

Ⓐ `1.4` **Logoso**

Hospital ❶ `7` `1.0` **Hospital** *info.*
O'Castelino
Opción `4.6` Fabrica
▲ 370m

Buxantes

Igrexa S. Eulalia Ⓐ**Xunta**
Truanes **As Carizas**

Concello *centro* `3.4` Ⓟ **O' Arxentino**
DUMBRIA

Cee ↘

< Vimianzo   Berdoias

C-552

río Fragoso   A Serpe   Cee ↗

C-552

Capela A Virxe do Espino
(Fonte Santa) †θ
Trasufre `3.1`

Río Castro   *río Castro*

Picola
Senande Coxa
O Cabanel 🅷Rego
A Grixa `4.5` **Vilatose**
✗   *Couciero*
θ
✗

E *Sunrise*   S

Capela S.Isodora†
Plaza
Quintáns `1.4` 🅷
Pedrajas Ⓒ†   *río San Martiño*
S.Martiño [+150m]
San Martiño Ⓐ `4.2` **Ozón**
Igrexa de S. Martiño   *río Negro*

Sunset

O

Paris
Ⓟ `2.0` **Os Muiños**
Praia de Lago 🅷   **Monasterio**
[+2 km]   Ⓐ*Igrexa S.Xulián*   *Finisterre ↗*
Merexo   **Moraime**
San Roque `3.2` †
Chorente

Bajuca
🅷

MUXÍA

CAMARIÑAS   Ⓐ `0.0` **Centro Bela Muxia**

Igrexa de St. Xulián de Moraime *XIc* [**0.8** km] adj. the church is the recently renovated monastery ●*Alb.* *Hs* **Monasterio de Moraime** *Priv.* *[38÷2]* €12 +4 €80 ℂ 881 076 055 *www.hostelmonasteriodemoraime.com* [*The original monastery established by Benedictine monks gave rise to the name 'land of monks' Mongía or Muxía*].

Continue diagonally over the park and take the steps down over main road again by ruined house onto rough path veering right> down to secondary road and up into **Os Muiños** [**1.2** km].

2.0 km **Os Muiños** *The Mills* small town with facilities. The waymarked route brings us behind the village to avoid the main road by turning up <left by *farmacia* and then down by *panadería* over the **río Negro** passing turn (left) to local river walk *paseo fluvial* and turn off (right) to café/pension •*P' **Paris** x4* €30 ℂ 981 740 616 on main road. Continue to end of village and turn <left in the direction of Merexo *(camping 5km **sign**)* [**0.4** km]. This quiet road meanders through pine forest to veer off **right**> [**1.4** km] [*Note: Merexo s/o •P' **Atlántico** x5* €35 ℂ 981 750 652 *+200m*]. The path turns up right> around side of house onto a wide forest track that winds its way up through dense pine woods around *Pena da Serra* alto (150m) continue s/o at cross of 5 tracks and turn <left on road in the aptly named **Vilar de Sobremonte** [**1.5** km]. The route now zig-zags sharp right> to the parish church of San Martiña de Ozón and the adj. monastery now coming back to life as an albergue [**0.9** km].

4.2 km **Monasterio San Martiño de Ozón** ●*Alb.* **San Martiño** *Asoc.* *[12÷2]* €-donation ℂ 981 750 707 XIIth century monastery & casa rectoral a collective venture largely made up of pilgrims who simply 'arrived and never left' mixed reports *(previously Aurora)*. Turn down <left by wayside cross onto an ancient cobbled street with one of Galicia's longest granaries *horreos*

XVIth with 22 pairs of granite supports which is also part of the albergue and now 'stores' volunteers working in the community. Short 150m detour (right) to ⛵ *San Martiño* on the main road. *Stay focused [!] this next stretch twists and turns its way into Quintáns but is generally well waymarked.* Continue over the **río San Martiño** and s/o track over road turning <left and imm. right> to wayside cross at **Lugar Pedragás** •*CR* **Casal Pedrajas** ℂ 689 946 940 *www. casalpedrajas.com* €80+ / ●*Alb.* **Et Suseia** *Priv.[10÷1]* €15 ℂ 689 946 940. S/o over road veering right past farm buildings into:

1.4 km **Quintáns Plaza Maior** town with good facilities on the AC-440 with several café/bars and lodging at ¶/•P˙ **Plaza** x7 €25-40 Ⓒ 981 750 452 (Isaac) *www.plazapension.com* in the main square. From here the path continues over the main road up past 🕭 *D'arriba* (right) and Capela S. Isodora (left) s/o at crossroads and imm. <left onto wide track keep s/o (ignoring paths to left or right) to top

of rise and s/o through eucalyptus woods and <left on **road** [**4.1** km] and next right> into **Vilastose** *A Grixa* [**0.4** km].

4.5 km **Vilatose** *A Grixa* ●*Alb.*O Cabanel *Priv.[12÷1]* €14 +1 €40 Ⓒ 600 644 879 (Raquel) *www.albergueocabanel.com* also ¶ *menú*. Igrexa S. Cibrán (separate bell tower) turn <left at crossroads into **Senande** [**0.7** km]. 🕭 *Bar-Tienda* Casa Rego turn right> at crossroads down the main street past 🕭 *Bar* A Picola and 🕭 *A Coxa* where Jesús will serve you a drink while his mother Pilar might cook you one of the best omelettes in Galicia! *Stay focused [!] on this next section our route criss-crosses several roads.* Just past the bar veer s/o <left onto minor road (pista polideportiva) and turn <**left** [**0.9** km] to T-junction imm. ahead and turn right> and continue along quiet road turning <left at next T-junction down over *Río Castro* [**1.1** km] (whose waters we crossed in Lires) and up to the roadside chapel in **Trasufre** [**0.4** km].

3.1 km **Trasufre** chapel of Our Lady of Espiño *Capela A Virxe do Espiño* (also known as Santuario de N.S de Aránzazu) and below it the Holy Fountain *Fonte Santa* whose waters are said to have healing powers. *[You will find pieces of cloth tied to the hedgerow here – a local tradition going back centuries whereby pilgrims come to this shrine for healing by leaving behind*

unwanted ailments to disintegrate along with the cloth that is their symbolic representation – do not tidy up!].

Follow the road up right past cruceiro and water tap (left) to turn off <**left** [**0.3** km] [!] onto track and imm. right> by modern horreo (red arrow) onto narrow path around the right hand (southerly) side of the hill. The path is steep but has been well surfaced and meanders through delightful woodland up to the main road [**1.3** km]. Here turn down <left on a path parallel to the main AC-552 to cross over [!] onto the old road over *Río Fragoso* up s/o at roundabout [**1.0** km] past bus-stop (left) veer right at next roundabout into the centre of Dumbría [**0.8** km].

3.4 km **Dumbría** *Centro Concello* with chronological display recording

the history of the area. Oppsite the Concello down side street is •*P' O Arxentino* *x7* €30-40 Ⓒ 981 744 051 with restaurant, bar and shop. Continue past the concello on main road *[Casa Curiña to the rear currently closed]*. 🍴/🛒*Bar-supermecado* Truanés also 🍴 *Bar Xacopeo*. **Dumbria:** A quiet administrative centre with a declining population currently 3,300. Daily bus connection to Santiago up to 4 times daily with change in Baio and journey time 2½ hours €10 – check schedule updates at Bar Truanés. Taxi service Jesús Ⓒ 647 236 701 ± I hour €80.

Continue along main road past ***Iglesia de Santa Eulalia*** (left) and down to the bottom of the hill and turn right> past play area and to the rear of the sports centre **polideportivo [0.6 km]** and ●*Alb.* **O Conco** *Xunta [26÷4]* €8 Ⓒ 981 744 001 (Concello de Dumbria) ultra modern pilgrim hostel with all facilities built with funds from Galician economic hero Amancio Ortega (see photo>). Keep s/o along wide track and take sharp turn right> onto path which emerges

at a crossroads ❖ *[Detour Castro right +400m •CR̈́́A Pichona x6* €60 Ⓒ 609 649 252 *www.casapichona. com all meals served]*. ❖ The camino continues s/o up into the hamlet of **As Carizas [1.0 km]** and imm. up sharp <left onto concrete path that shortly continues as steep pathway through woodland and turn right> on **main road [0.2 km]** (*not* path s/o). Beware of traffic on the dangerous bend [!] and turn up <**left [0.4 km]** onto woodland path to cross back over main road again and over the headwaters of the *rio Fragoso*, now little more than a trickle, and back up to **main road [1.1 km]**.   Now it's all the way back to the factory at Hospital visible on the horizon and option point [**1.3** km].

4.6 km Option / Crossroads. *Note: This is the original option point to Finisterre or Muxía.* If you have walked from Santiago as part of the camino Finisterre / Muxía circuit the route will now appear familiar as we return to Santiago from this point *in reverse*: Pass 🍴/*Alb.* O' Castelino (*details below*) [**0.6** km] down to Hospital [**0.4**km].

1.0 km **Hospital** Pilgrim information centre on main road. ▲ *[Detour 300m to ●Alb.* **Hospital** *Priv.[20÷3]* €14 Ⓒ 981 747 387 *continue **down** main road and cross over into the village. The hostel is located at the lower end]*. ▲ To continue turn right> and imm. <left at info. centre down into Logoso:

1.4 km Logoso ☕ /●*Alb.* Logoso *Priv.[32÷4]* €15 *+10* €30-40 Ⓒ 659 505 399. *[The family also run the nearby apartments at A Pedra Ⓒ 652 864 623 x5 apt./rooms from €35-55 on main road +0.6 km].* Continue down over *río do Hospital* and along the forest track back down over *Rego do Santa Lucia* and up past the casa rural •*Pr***As Pías** *x4* €40-60 Ⓒ 981 741 520 m: 617 026 005 to the central hostels in Olveiroa.

3.5 km Olveiroa *Centro [see page p.41 for list of accommodation].*

Note ❶ maps in these guides are one-directional so the reverse maps *back* to Santiago are included on the next two pages for those intending to return by foot via Negreira.

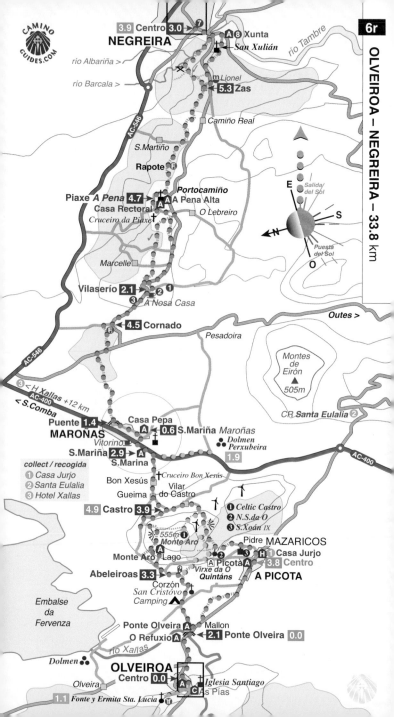

CAMINO
GUIDES.COM

3.9 Centro **3.0**
NEGREIRA

A 8 Xunta
San Xulián

río Albariña >

río Barcala >

río Tambre

m Lionel

5.3 Zas

Camiño Real

S.Martiño

Rapote

Portocamiño
Piaxe A Pena **4.7** A Pena Alta
Casa Rectoral
Cruceiro da Piaxe
O Lebreiro

E
Salida/del Sol
S
N
O
Puesta del Sol

Marcelle

Vilaserío **2.1**
A Nosa Casa

Outes >

4.5 Cornado

Pesadoira

Montes de Eirón
▲ 505m

3 < H Xallas +12 km
AC-400
< S.Comba

Puente **1.4**
MAROÑAS
Vitorino
S.Mariña **2.9**
S.Marina

Casa Pepa
0.6 S.Mariña *Maroñas*
Dolmen
Perxubeira

1.9

CR Santa Eulalia **2**

collect / recogida
1 Casa Jurjo
2 Santa Eulalia
3 Hotel Xallas

† *Cruceiro Bon Xesús*
Bon Xesús
Vilar
do Castro
Gueima

4.9 Castro **3.9**

1 Celtic Castro
2 N.S.da O
3 S.Xoán IX

555m
Monte Aro

Pidre MAZARICOS

2
A Picota
3 **H** **1** Casa Jurjo
3.8 Centro

Monte Aro Lago

Abeleiroas **3.3**

Virxe da O
A PICOTA
Quintáns

Corzón
San Cristóvo
Camping ▲

Embalse da Fervenza

Ponte Olveira **A** Mallon
O Refuxio **A** **2.1** Ponte Olveira **0.0**

río Xallas

Dolmen ●●
Olveira

OLVEIROA
Centro **0.0**
A *Iglesia Santiago*
C As Pías

1.1 *Fonte y Ermita Sta. Lucia* †

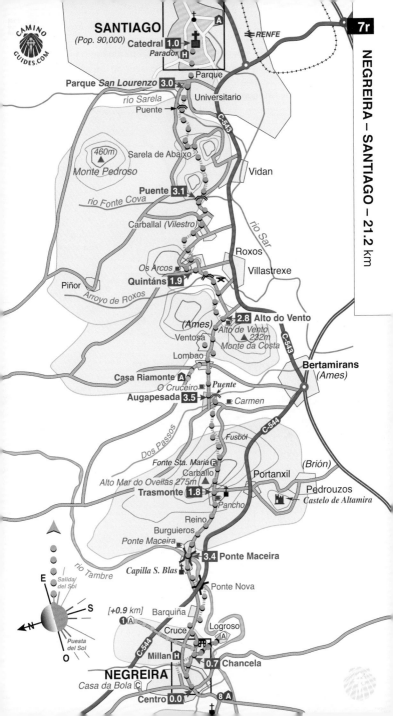

CAMINO GUIDES.COM

SANTIAGO
(Pop. 90,000) Catedral 1.0
Parador
A
H
RENFE

Parque San Lourenzo 3.0
río Sarela
Puente
Parque
Universitario
C-543

460m
Monte Pedroso
Sarela de Abaixo
Vidan

río Fonte Cova
Puente 3.1

Carballal *(Vilestro)*
río Sar
Roxos
Villastrexe

Os Arcos
Quintáns 1.9
Piñor
Arroyo de Roxos

(Ames)
Ventosa
Alto do Vento 2.8
Alto de Vento
▲ 232m
Monte da Costa

Lombao
Bertamirans
(Ames)
C-543

Casa Riamonte A
O Cruceiro
Puente
Augapesada 3.5
Carmen
C-544

Dos Passos
Fusból
(Brión)

Fonte Sta. María
Carballo ▲
Portanxil
Pedrouzos
Castelo de Altamira

Alto Mar do Ovellas 275m
Trasmonte 1.8
Pancho

Reino
Burguieros
Ponte Maceira
Ponte Maceira 3.4

Capilla S. Blas
Ponte Nova

E
*Salida/
del Sol*
S
río Tambre
[+0.9 km]
Barquiña
1 A
Logroso
A
N
*Puesta
del Sol*
O
Cruce
Millan H
Chancela 0.7

NEGREIRA
Casa da Bola C
Centro 0.0
8 A

The following maps are for those pilgrims walking the circuit in the alternative *anti-clockwise* direction; from Olveiroa (Hospital) to Muxía *[map 5a]* – Muxía to Finisterre *[map 4a]* – Finisterre to Olveiroa *[map 3a]*. Details of accommodation are listed in the appropriate pages as in the clockwise journey.

5a–3a Olveiroa (Hospital) – Muxía – Finisterre

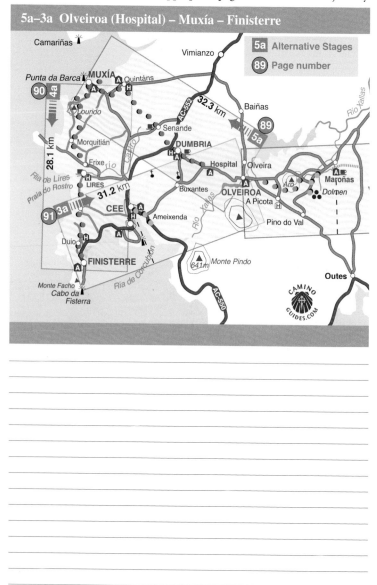

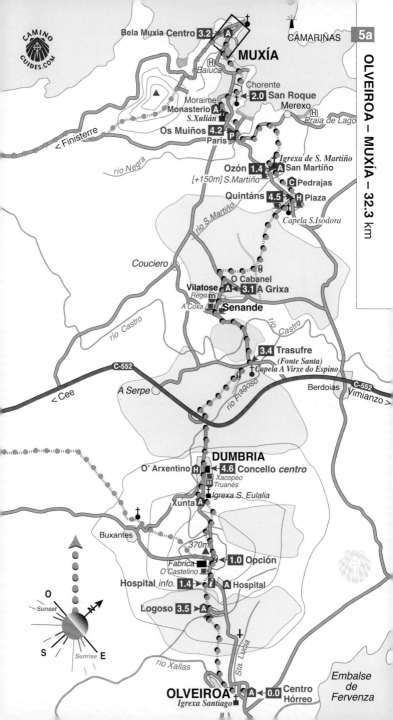

CAMINO GUIDES.COM

CAMARIÑAS

Bela Muxia Centro **3.2** ◀ A †

MUXÍA

Baiuca H

Chorente

2.0 ◀ **San Roque**
Merexo

H
Praia de Lago

Moraime
Monasterio A †
S.Xulián
Os Muiños **4.2** †
Paris P

< Finisterre

rio Negra

† *Igrexa de S. Martiño*
Ozón **1.4** A **San Martiño**
[+150m] *S.Martiño*
C **Pedrajas**
Quintáns **4.5** H **Plaza**

Capela S.Isodora

rio S.Martiño

Couciero

θ

O Cabanel
Vilatose A **3.1** **A Grixa**
Rego m
A Coxa **Senande**

rio Castro

< Cee

rio Castro

3.4 **Trasufre**
(Fonte Santa)
† *Capela A Virxe do Espino*

C-552

A Serpe
rio Fragoso

Berdoias
C-552
Vimianzo >

DUMBRIA
O' Arxentino H **4.6** **Concello** *centro*
▥ *Xacopeo Truanés*
Xunta A † **Igrexa S. Eulalia**

Buxantes †

370m
▲
Fabrica ? **1.0** **Opción**
O'Castelino
Hospital *info.* **1.4** ? A **Hospital**

Logoso **3.5** A

rio Xallas
Sta. Lucia

OLVEIROA †
Igrexa Santiago
A **0.0** **Centro**
Hórreo

Embalse de Fervenza

O
Sunset
N
S
E
Sunrise

CAMINO GUIDES.COM

FINISTERRE `A` `1.1` **Centro** *Xunta*
(Pop. 4,900)

Praia de Mar do Fora

`4a`

Baixamar

`3.1` **Arenal**

Praia de Langosteira

San Martiño Duio

Trebol

Anchoa

Hermedesuxo

C-552

Mallas

Castro

San Salvador `2.6` `H`

Dugium

Sardiñeiro

Castromiñán

Rial

Sinfín

Buxán `4.3` `A`

Castrexe

Praia de Rostro

Corcubión

Padrís

Cee

C-554

Canosa `2.4`

C-552

Ría de Lires

As Eiras `A`

Playa

Lires `2.0` `C` *A Braña*

Cabanas

Porcar

Praia de Nemiña

Pontenova

Kiosco

Casa Ceferinos `C` `3.9` **Frixe**

Frixe *Abaixo*

Nemiña

O Muiño

Touriñán

Guisamonde

Vilachán

Fuente / Cruceiro †`F`

Viseo

Morquintián `3.0`

Cabo Touriñan

Alto `3.3` *270m* ▲ Alto

Monte Lourido ▲ *310m*

Xurarantes `F`

Os Muiños

`H` *Parador Spa*

Opción / Vista `2.4`

Praia Lourido

San Roque †

MUXÍA `A`

Centro `0.0` `A`

S

Sunset

Sunrise *O*

E

MUXÍA – FINISTERRE – 28.1 km

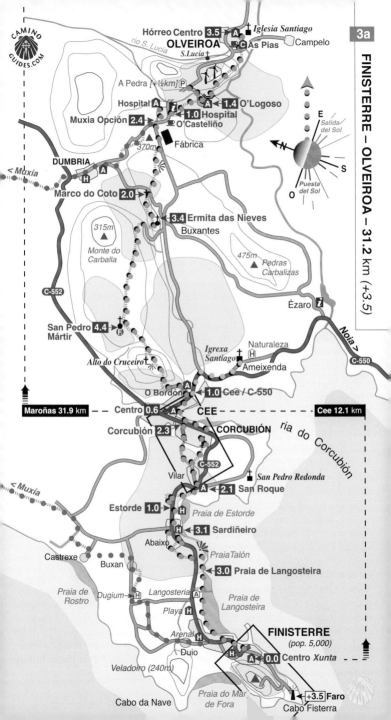

RETURNING HOME: *Some inner thoughts ...*

Regardless of how far you have walked it is possible that your outer appearance might have changed, it is also possible that the way we perceive the world has gone through some metamorphosis. This inner transformation may well deepen as the lessons we learnt along the way become more fully integrated. While an obvious purpose of pilgrimage is to bring about an inner shift, it is also possible that our familiar world will no longer support this inner change. This realisation might engender different emotions as we come to see that choices may have to be made that could alter our previous way of life – what we do, where we work, who we live with, our social circuit, where and how we pray or meditate. Indeed the whole purpose, focus and direction of our life may have altered. This may be intimidating to those who previously knew us *the way we were.* Change threatens the status quo but the biggest challenge may be to hold fast to our new understanding garnered from the insights we learnt along the way.

Whatever our individual experiences it is likely that we will be in a heightened state of consciousness and sensitivity. We should resist squeezing our itinerary and the feeling we need to rush back into our usual pattern of work and general lifestyle – this can be a crucial moment. How often do we witness change in ourselves and others only to see fear come and rob us of our new understanding and orientation. Perhaps this is the time to revisit the Self-assessment questionnaire and recall the original purpose and intention of our pilgrimage. If this was (for example) to 'come closer to God', then we should not be surprised if everything that could get in the way of that high invocation is removed from our life, or at least challenged!

Essentially, we are all on a journey of rediscovery of our Essential Nature – our spiritual reality as we begin opening to the knowledge of Higher Worlds. Remember that we have collectively been asleep a long time. While change *can* happen in the twinkling of an eye, it is often experienced as a slow and painful process. The main challenge to our new perspective is likely to be the twin demons of fear and lethargy. The extent to which we hold onto a new way of looking at the world is measured by how far we are prepared to hold onto our truth in the face of opposition – often from those who profess to love us – by such was Christ crucified.

Of course our inner changes may not be so dramatic or those around us may likewise be engaged in inner work and so, far from feeling threatened, may welcome your shift with open arms and hearts – in this case you are blessed indeed. However, it would still be well to remember that these supportive others may not have spent weeks walking an ancient spiritual path surrounded by the silence of nature. Take time to integrate back into your life and nurture yourself. Build up a network of fellow pilgrims who can empathise with how you might be feeling and can actively support you.

Know that change is nearly always seen as threat within consensus society. Know also that if you try and change another to your new viewpoint you can aggravate the sense of loss and alienation felt by that other – this is all part of the journey and grist for the mill. Ultimately you can only be responsible for your own actions and re-actions. You cannot be responsible for the experience of others.

This guidebook is dedicated to awakening beyond human consciousness. It was born out of an existential crisis and the perceived need for a time to reflect on the purpose of life and its direction. Collectively devoid of inner-connectedness and a sense of the sacred, we live in a spiritual vacuum of our own making. While ensnared by our outer-directed materialistic world, we unwittingly hold the key to the door of our self-made prison. We can walk free any time we choose. We have been so long separated from our divine origins that we have forgotten what freedom feels like. In our fear of the unknown we choose to limit the potential of each new day to the familiarity of our prison surroundings. Perhaps *El Camino* will reveal the key to your own inner awakening.

As you take a well deserved rest at the end of the long road to the end of the way the question might well arise, 'Is the journey over or just beginning?' Whatever answer you receive will doubtless be right for you at this time. I wish you well in your search for the Truth and your journey Home and extend my humble blessings to a fellow pilgrim on the path and leave you with the words of *J R R Tolkein* from The Lord of the Rings:

> *The Road goes ever on and on*
> *Down from the door where it began.*
> *Now far ahead the Road has gone,*
> *And I must follow, if I can,*
> *Pursuing it with wary feet,*
> *Until it joins some larger way,*
> *Where many paths and errands meet.*
> *And whither then? I cannot say.*

❖

A tithe of all royalties from the sale of this book will be distributed to individuals or organisations seeking to preserve the physical and spiritual integrity of this route.

The breeze at dawn has something to tell you. Don't go back to sleep. Rumi

Much of the information given here comes from local information garnered along the way. Myth and legend abound and, while frequently arising from some historical occurrence they are, by their very nature, not dependent on fact. If you are interested to find additional sources that referred to the importance of Finisterre as a place of spiritual transformation – try your local library or search the internet.

The Bible in Spain, by George Borrow. Originally published London, 1842

A Stranger in Spain, by H.V Morton. Methuen: London, 1955.

Nine Faces of Christ, by Eugene Whitworth. DeVorss 1993.

A Course In Miracles, Foundation for Inner Peace. Penguin Books 1975

Poems – Rosalía de Castro, translated by Anna-Marie Aldaz, Barbara N. Gantt and Anne C. Bromley. State University of New York Press, 1991.

As Pegadas de Santiago na Cultura de Fisterra, by Benjamin Trillo Trillo. Fundación Caixa Galicia, 1999. (Trilingual: Galego, Castellano, English)

O Camiño de Fisterra, by Fernando Alonso Romero. Ediciòns Xerais de Galicia, 1993 (Trilingual: Galego, Castellano, English)

Mar Tenebroso – A costa da morte do sol, Ramón Allegue Martínez. EuroGraficas pichel,1996. (Galego)

Galicia Enteira – Fisterra e Costa da Morte, Xosé Luís Laredo Verdejo. Ediciòns Xerais de Galicia, 1996. (Galego)

El Camino del Milenio, Ramón Allegue Martínez. Baupres Editores, 2000.

O Camiño dos Peregrinos á Fin do Mundo, Antón Pombo y otros. Deputación Provincial da Coruña, 2000. (Galego)

The Fisterra-Muxía Way, Manuel Rodríguez. Xunta de Galicia,

There are many paths back to our divine origins and many routes to Santiago. If you have walked the popular Camino Francés or Finisterre and are considering another camino — you might consider exploring one of the alternative pathways which would help disperse the environmental and commercial impact across all routes.

PILGRIM ASSOCIATIONS:
UK: The Confraternity of St. James +44 [0]2079 289 988 e-mail: *office@csj.org.uk* website: *www.csj.org.uk* with online bookshop.
IRELAND: The Camino Society Ireland. Based in Dublin: *www.caminosociety.ie*
U.S.A. American Pilgrims on the Camino. *www.americanpilgrims.org*
CANADA: Canadian Company of Pilgrims Canada. *www.santiago.ca*
SOUTH AFRICA: Confraternity of St. James of SA *www.csjofsa.za.org*
AUSTRALIA: Australian Friends of the Camino *www.afotc.org*

SANTIAGO:
Pilgrim Office *oficinadelperegrino.com/en*
Tourism: *www.santiagoturismo.com*
Luggage storage & transfer / forum & meeting space *www.casaivar.com*
Backpack storage & local tours *pilgrim.es* Rúa Nova, 7 (adj. cathedral)

PILGRIM WEBSITES: (in English) loosely connected with the Way of St. James or with the theme of pilgrimage that you may find helpful.

Camino News: Largest English online camino forum *www.caminodesantiago.me*
Alternatives of St. James: *www.alternatives.org.uk* Exploration of ways of living that honour all spiritual traditions. Based at St. James Church, London.
The British Pilgrimage Trust: *www.britishpilgrimage.org*
Gatekeeper Trust *www.gatekeeper.org.uk*
Findhorn Foundation personal/planetary transformation *www.findhorn.org*
Lucis Trust education, meditation and World Goodwill *www.lucistrust.org*
Paulo Coelho reflections from author of The Pilgrimage *paulocoelhoblog.com*
Peace Pilgrim Her life and work *www.peacepilgrim.com*
The Quest A Guide to the Spiritual Journey *www.thequest.org.uk*

ALBERGUE, HOSTAL AND HOTEL BOOKING SITES:
List of albergues open in Winter: *www.aprinca.com/alberguesinvierno/*
Albergues: *www.onlypilgrims.com/en*
Hostals: *www.hostelworld.com*
Paradores: *www.parador.es*
Hotels: *www.booking.com*
B&Bs: *www.airbnb*
Christian Hospitality Network: *http://en.ephatta.com*

PILGRIM AND BACKPACK TRANSFERS / STORES:
Spanish Postal Service: *www.elcaminoconcorreos.com/en*
Camino Store Pamplona: *www.caminoteca.com/en*
Blog: Luggage and People Transport *www.amawalker.blogspot.co.uk*
St. Jean / Biarritz: *www.expressbourricot.com*
Roncesvalles to Sarria: *www.jacotrans.com*
Sarria to Santiago: *www.xacotrans.com*
All routes: *www.pilbeo.com/en*

12 Caminos de Santiago

❶ Camino Francés* 778 km
St. Jean – Santiago
Camino Invierno*
Ponferrada – Santiago **275 km**

❷ Chemin de Paris 1000 km
Paris – St. Jean via Tours

❸ Chemin de Vézelay 900 km
Vezélay – St. Jean via Bazas

❹ Chemin du Puy 740 km
Le Puy-en-Velay – St. Jean
Ext. to Geneva, Budapest

❺ Chemin d'Arles 750 km
Arles – Somport Pass
Camino Aragonés **160 km**
Somport Pass – Óbanos
Camí San Jaume **600 km**
Port de Selva – Jaca
Camino del Piamonte **515 km**
Narbonne - Lourdes - St. Jean

❻ Camino de Madrid 320 km
Madrid – Sahagún

Camino de Levante 900 km
Valencia – Zamora
Alt. via Cuenca – Burgos

❼ Camino Mozárabe 390 km
Granada – Mérida
(Málaga alt. via Baena)

❽ Via de la Plata 1,000 km
Seville – Santiago
Camino Sanabrés Ourense **110 km**

❾ Camino Portugués *Central** **640 km**
Lisboa – Porto 389 km
Porto – Santiago 251 km
Camino Portugués *Costa** **320 km**
Porto – Santiago
via Caminha & **Variante Espiritual***

❿ Camino Finisterre* 86 km
Santiago – Finisterre
via – Muxía – Santiago **114 km**

⓫ Camino Inglés* 120 km
Ferrol & Coruna – Santiago

⓬ Camino del Norte 830 km
Irún – Santiago via Gijón
Camino Primitivo 320 km
Oviedo – Lugo – Melide